Bureaucratic Language in Government and Business

Bureaucratic Language in Government and Business

ROGER W. SHUY

GEORGETOWN UNIVERSITY PRESS / WASHINGTON D.C.

Georgetown University Press, Washington, D.C.

Printed in the Unites States of America

10 9 8 7 6 5 4 3 2 1 1998

THIS VOLUME IS PRINTED ON ACID-FREE OFFSET BOOK PAPER

Library of Congress Cataloging-in-Publication Data

Shuy, Roger W.
Bureaucratic language in government and business / Roger W. Shuy.
p. cm.
Includes index.
1. Bureaucracy—Language. 2. Bureaucracy—United States—Language. I. Title.
JF1501.S48 1998
351—dc21
ISBN 0-87840-696-4. — ISBN 0-87840-697-2 (pbk.) 98-5664

Contents

Foreword ix

Acknowledgments xv

Chapter 1
Trying to Do Conversation on Paper: A Case Study of a Medicare Benefits Notice 1

Background 2, The Original Form Sent to Beneficiaries 4, Problems with the Original Explanation of Medicare Benefits 8, HHS's Response to the Court Order to Revise the Form 12, Further Suggestions for Revision 14, Problems with a Paper Hearing 14, Failure to Capture Beneficiaries' Perspective 16, Futility of Follow-up Telephone Communication 17, Resolution of the Case 17

Chapter 2
Training a Bureaucracy to Write Clearly: A Case Study of the Social SecurityAdministration 19

Congress Mandates the Social Security Administration to Notify Beneficiaries about Supplemental Security Income 19,

Revision of SSA's Attempt to Comply with This Mandate 21, SSA's Request That We Train Their Notice-Writing Staff 24, Preparations by SSA 24, Early Ethnographic Observations 25, Designing the Training Program 27, The Training Program 28, Features of the Training Program 29, Fieldwork 29, Topic Analysis 31, The Decision Tree 34, Speech Acts 34, Discourse Analysis 39, Word Comprehension 42, Authority Based on Linguistic Justification 43, Conclusion 44

Chapter 3

A Bureaucracy's Struggle with Saying "No": A Medicare Case Study 46

Being Denied a Claim for Medicare 46, Title 47, Sentence Structure 49, Conveyed Meaning 51, Conclusion 52

Chapter 4

When Bureaucracies Clash: A Case Study of Physicians' Disability Report Forms 53

The Clash of Bureaucracies 53, TDDS's Proposed Medical Assessment Report Form 54, Legal Services Revised Form B 57, Legal Services Revised Form C 62, Conclusion 62

Chapter 5

Bureaucratic Speech: Research on Telephone vs. In-Person Administrative Hearings 63

Background 64, Opinion Survey 66, Analysis of Actual Hearings 67, Power in the Administrative Hearing 69, Status and Role in Administrative Hearings 70, Hearings with Physicians 70, Hearings with Attorneys 71, Hearings with Beneficiaries 72, Strategy 1: Rely on Informal, Conversational Style 73, Strategy 2: Share (or give up) Perceived Power 81, Strategy 3: Letting the Beneficiaries Self-Generate Topics 88, Strategy 4: Defusing the Legal Format 89, Strategy 5: Taking the Beneficiary's Perspective 92, Strategy 6: Avoiding Displays of Knowledge 94, Advantages and Disadvantages of the Hearing Formats 97, Gender Differences 103, Socially Acquired Gender Specification 104, Physical Presence vs. Presence of Telephonic Voice Only 106, Conclusion 107

Chapter 6
Facing the Bureaucratic Language of the Insurance Industry: A Case Study of a Consumers' Affairs Conference 108

Aspects of Language that Contribute to Comprehensibility 113, Misconceptions about Language that Interfere with Comprehensibility 119, Conclusion 123

Chapter 7
Untangling the Bureaucratic Language of Real Estate: A Case Study of Commission Agreements 125

Background 126, Commission Agreement Number One 127, Commission Agreement Number Two 130, Commission Agreement Number Three 134, Discourse Analysis 137, Contrastive Analysis 140, Conclusion 142

Chapter 8
Attacking the Bureaucratic Language of Car Sales: A Case Study of a Car Sales Event 144

Background 145, Specialization of Functions 146, Adherence to Fixed Rules 150, Hierarchy of Authority 153, Conclusion 157

Chapter 9
Bureaucratic Language and Product Warning Labels: Case Studies of the Requirements of FDA and OSHA 158

Bureaucratic Language and Warnings 158, Bureaucratic Language and the U.S. Food and Drug Administration 159, Bureaucratic Language and the U.S. Occupational Safety and Health Administration (OSHA) 165, Conclusion 173

Chapter 10
What Is Bureaucratic Language and What Can Be Done About It? 175

What Is Bureaucratic Language? 176, What Can Be Done About Bureaucratic Language? 181

Works Cited 185

Index 187

Foreword

Who has not been puzzled, even stymied, by awkwardly phrased messages put forth by a bureaucracy? In the honest attempt to communicate with the American people, those enjoined with the task of writing public documents often sink into a verbal quagmire, out of which they cannot seem to climb. English teachers have railed about such bad writing for decades, and rightly so, but little progress seems to have been made by bureaucratic communications.

Educational advances, such as achieving clarity in the bureaucratic writing of government and industry, seldom stem from logic, from clear evidence of need, or from any desire for esthetic beauty. The English teaching profession seems to have placed its hopes on bureaucracies coming to understand the illogic of poor writing and on their somehow being able to instill a desire for language effectiveness, if not beauty, in the documents coming out of public places. But these hopes have been put forth for decades with little evidence of significant improvement. In fact, if one were to agree with today's language nay-sayers, things have actually gotten worse in recent years. On the other hand, a ray of hope can be found in some of the case studies reported here. It is a hope forged out of a growing alliance between law and linguistics, law providing the forum, threat, and power for change, and linguistics providing the methods and justification. Neither field, working alone, can be as effective as their combined effort.

One motivation for the bureaucracies to clean up their language act is that of economic cost effectiveness. Things seem to get changed in this world when economic issues raise their ugly heads. This should not be too surprising to a society that is beginning to see the attack on outrageous medical fees start to make small cracks in consumer costs. The last chapter in this saga has not yet been written, of course, but the advent of managed care seems to be the harbinger of some type of consumer relief. Meanwhile, those who have held power in such matters are beginning to encounter public relations problems. Similar resentment against millionaire athletes and CEOs is possibly not far behind.

But, one might argue, bureaucracies can hardly be considered in the same way as fields such as medicine, corporate management, and professional athletics. In a financial sense, this is quite true. But bureaucracies have had the status of impenetrability, much like medicine and sports. Walled by a heirarchy of authority, specialization of functions, adherence to fixed rules, complexity, physical isolation, and an administrative structure marked by officialdom, red tape, and proliferation, bureaucracies cannot be touched easily. But a few brave souls and a few diligent organizations have begun to be successful in bringing about healthy language changes in some of our bureaucratic institutions. And when this has happened, the attack has been economically based, largely through lawsuits or research that brings to light the unnecessary perpetuation of overly complex and arcane prose and finds a way to make such prose costly to the institution that dares to use it.

Although various legal avenues have been the major source of the changes that have come about so far, attorneys are not doing this alone. Recently they have called upon linguists to help them. In that I have been one of the linguists who has analyzed bureaucratic language in such settings, this book calls upon this work to exemplify some of the ways in which my field has, and can be, of assistance in such matters. It is my belief that by sharing what we have done in various cases, in research, and in conferences on bureaucratic language issues, the intersection of law and linguistics may be furthered. It is hoped that attorneys will more and more come to realize that linguistics is their useful ally. It is equally hoped that linguists who have not yet had access to this field will find it attractive enough for them to make their own contributions that will go far beyond that which is described here. Finally, it is hoped that bureaucracies themselves may use the information offered here for their own benefit and to improve their own communication. There are no secrets here. One basic requirement of educators is to give their ideas away, not to hide them from others. Although the work described here begins with a linguist working on one side or the other of a given bureaucratic issue, side-taking is not its point. Language is analyzed from a neutral position. Language is what it is, and it does not matter on which side of a legal case the linguist works. It is the legal system of advocacy that causes experts to work on one side or the other, not the training, beliefs, or ideas of linguistics.

Most of this book documents a modest impact of linguistic analysis that grew out of attacks on the economic well-being of various segments of bureaucracies. Through the efforts of the National Senior Citizens Law Center (NSCLC, also known as the Gray Panthers), for example, class action suits were brought against various branches of the U. S. Department of Health and Human Services (HHS), later called Health, Education, and Welfare (HEW), providing the setting in four of the chapters in this book, all of which address the unsatisfactory language used by these bureaucracies.

Chapter 1 describes the Medicare bureaucracy's effort to replace actual, face-to-face hearings with what they referred to as "paper hearings." Can written communication offer the same benefits as oral? Perhaps overwhelmed by increasing costs and decreasing resources, Medicare tried to substitute "paper hearings" for face-to-face encounters, much to the objection of consumer advocates.

Successful in this effort, the Gray Panthers next attacked the Social Security Administration's (SSA) response to a Congressional mandate to notify all recipients of Social Security that they might also be eligible for Supplemental Security Income (SSI). This battle was won by SSA in a Supreme Court decision, having just been lost at the district and appellate levels. Chapter 2 describes my work in this case, first with the Gray Panthers in their lawsuit and then, after switching sides, in training SSA notice-writers to write more effective notices.

Chapter 3 is another case study of my work with the Gray Panthers, again with SSA as the offending party. It deals with the problems this bureacracy had in denying recipients' claims and how difficult it is for bureacracies to say "no" effectively and gracefully.

However easy it is to think of a single abstract entity such as "the bureaucracy," there are actually many of them and sometimes different bureaucracies bump heads over language. Chapter 4 describes such a clash between the bureaucratic language of a state bureaucracy with the bureaucracy of the medical profession.

Various government agencies face the uneasy constant pressures of the need to cut back financially, causing them to try to think up new ways to streamline their operations. One such attempt is focussed on the effort to reduce administrative hearings of SSA or Medicare recipients who have had their claims rejected. For years, efforts have been made to replace in-person hearings with telephonic substitutions. Once again, the National Senior Citizens Law Center entered the battle, enlisting the aid of linguistic research to determine the pros and cons of each method of conducting administrative hearings. Chapter 5 details the procedures and findings of this linguistic research into this controversy about bureaucratic language.

When Jimmy Carter was president, he evidenced great sympathy for the need to improve bureaucratic language and made possible the creation of the Document Design Project of the American Institutes for Research in Washington, D.C., originally funded heavily by the government but now largely existing with independent resources. It was intended to serve government bureaucracies and private business alike. One of the early governmental thrusts was an attempt to improve the langage of the insurance business, both in regulations and in company policies. Toward that end, the U.S. Office of Consumer Affairs held a conference in 1978 to face head-on some of the issues of unclear language. Chapter 6 of this book describes the attempt to supply linguistic knowledge in this cause.

The bureaucratic language of real estate provides another example of the way business emulates government in the perpetuation of ambiguous and complex prose. Sometimes such language gets so out of hand that the only way to untangle it is to call on a linguist to figure it out. Such a case is described in Chapter 7.

Not always can we define a bureaucracy as a government office or agency. Bureaucracies exist in business and industry as well, although we do not always think of them in this way. Even individual businesses, such as real estate, automobile dealers, and commercial manufacturers, exist in a heavily bureaucratic environment. "Bureaucrat" is commonly defined as "an official who works by fixed routine without exercising intelligent judgment," and "bureaucracy" is defined as "excessive multiplication of, and concentration of power in, administrative bureaus or administrators," and "administration characterized by excessive red tape and routine." Chapter 8 deals with the routinized, unthinking bureaucratic force of a Texas car dealership against a naive deaf man who came into the dealership to price, not to purchase, a car. The deaf man's attorney used linguistic analysis to achieve a settlement against the dealership.

The U.S. Food and Drug Administration (FDA) provides guidelines for manufacturers to follow in writing warning labels for their products. No industry wants to believe that its products are unsafe or dangerous, so there is a constant tension between the actual wordings chosen by the manufacturer and the wordings specified in the FDA and Occupational Safety and Health Administration (OSHA) guidelines. Chapter 9 in this book describes a linguistic analysis of these guidelines in relationship to a product's ultimate warning labels.

Chapters 1 through 5 focus on governmental bureaucracies while chapters 6 through 9 deal with bureaucratic language found in business and industry. Obviously, not all governmental bureaucracies are dealt with here. Such would be a monumental task. Nor do we examine all the bureaucracies of business and industry, for essentially the same reason. For that reason, the book is inductive rather than programmatic or theoretical; the cases described are limited to those for which actual experience has provided the stimulus and data. Nevertheless, there is a common thread throughout these cases that illustrates the basic features of bureaucratic language.

The cases delineated here also provide a bit of variety in terms of structure. Two cases (Chapters 1 and 5) describe research that grew out of a problem facing a large number of government bureacracies as they tried to streamline and cut costs. Another case (Chapter 2) is a description of a training program that grew out of a lawsuit lost by a government agency. One case (Chapter 6) describes a government-sponsored conference on a bureaucratic language issue. Two cases depict what happens when two bureaucracies clash (Chapters 4 and 9). The other cases relate to actual lawsuits, or projected ones, brought about by advocates against various agencies and businesses. Like all case studies, it is difficult, if not dangerous, to make sweeping generalizations from them. They are what they are, actual events in recent times.

In the final chapter (Chapter 10), effort is made to define bureaucratic language based on the experiences and findings of these previous cases, training programs, and research findings. An attempt is made to understand bureaucratic language, and suggestions are offered to improve it.

Chapters 2, 7, 8, and 9 have antecedents in work that I have published in the past, although the current treatment expands them considerably and has a different focus. It should be noted, however, that the original articles and the current chapters make use of much of the same data. Specifically, Chapter 2 is based on my article, "Changing Language Policy in a Bureaucracy," which was published in *Language Spread and Language Policy* (Peter Lowenberg, ed. 1988). Chapter 7 has antecedents in my chapter, "Linguistic Analysis of Real Estate Commission Agreements in a Civil Law Suit," published in *Language Topics: Essays in Honour of Michael Halliday*, Ross Steel and Terry Threadgold, eds. 1987. Chapter 8 makes use of some of the data described in my article, "Deceit, Distress, and False Imprisonment: The Anatomy of a Car Sales Event," *Forensic Linguistics*, 1994. Chapter 9 relates to part of my article, "WarningLabels: Language, Law, and Comprehensibility," in *American Speech*, 1990.

Acknowledgments

My heartfelt thanks go to the attorneys who involved me in the cases described in this book, to my Georgetown graduate students who always inspired me, to my Georgetown faculty colleagues who supported and nurtured me, and to Georgetown University itself, which provided my academic home for thirty years.

Chapter 1

Trying to Do Conversation on Paper: A Case Study of a Medicare Benefits Notice

The problems that bureaucracies have with language issues often end up in courts of law. In 1979, the Gray Panthers brought a class action suit against Richard Schweiker, secretary of the U.S. Department of Health and Human Services (HHS), challenging the procedures for resolving disputes concerning program benefits of less than $100 (D.C. Civil Action No. 77-488). HHS contended that a "paper hearing" met the constitutional requirements of due process for the resolution of such disputes. The Gray Panthers disagreed, saying that nothing less than a full, formal, oral evidentiary hearing would satisfy due process guarantees. The district court found in favor of HHS. This decision was appealed by the Gray Panthers (Docket No. 79-1603), argued on April 28, 1980 and decided on March 18, 1981. The appellate court, as revealed in the decision of Judge Wald, argued that due process in such disputes "requires a procedure that lies somewhere between the two extremes presented by the parties." The court did not find it unconstitutional that Congress had eliminated the beneficiary right of a formal hearing in disputes over benefits of less than $100, but it did find that HHS's current interpretation of the Medicare Act gives insufficient protection of the appellant's due process rights. With that opinion, the court reversed the district court's decision but remanded the case to allow the court, with the assistance of HHS and the Gray Panthers, to revise the regulations in such a way as to satisfy due process considerations. In short, the court ruled that the "paper hearing" currently in use was inadequate and should be cured by a joint effort of both plaintiff and defendant.

Background

For those unfamiliar with the history of this issue, it may be helpful to point out that Congress had been concerned with the fact that beneficiaries of Medicare who were denied services by HHS had no personal forum for resolution of their complaints if their claims were under $1,000. As the Medicare bill was first reported out of the House Ways and Means Committee in 1965, there would have been a $1,000 limitation on formal hearing rights (H.R. Rep. No. 213, 89th Cong., 47 (1965). When the bill reached the Senate, however, Senator Edward Kennedy proposed that the amount be reduced to $100. Through his tireless efforts, a compromise solution was reached: denials of claims over $100 were entitled to an oral hearing but claims under $100 were entitled only to a paper explanation. In proposing his amendment to the U.S. Senate, Kennedy said the following:

> Mr. President, under all the laws passed by Congress dealing with public assistance and social welfare, Congress has never included any limitation upon the right of a citizen to appeal an administrative decision by the agency involved. In public assistance statutes we have always provided for the right of the beneficiary to question a decision made in his specific case, on the basis that the rules and regulations established to administer such laws cannot account for every possible situation where a real inequity may arise. While it may well be that many appeals will arise under public assistance laws as a result of misunderstanding of the benefits available and their accounts, we have nevertheless considered it important to keep the appeals route open so that valid complaints could be found and heard.
>
> I can fully realize the concerns that the Social Security Administration may have over the number of cases that may arise under this new statute, but I am convinced that until the Medicare program has been in operation for some time we should not place administrative ease above the rights of our elderly to question adverse decisions. To the majority of the elderly the amount in question may well involve a substantial part of their income or savings.
>
> Utilization review committees are also provided for in the bill and each hospital must have a review plan. While these wise

> provisions will be instrumental in controlling the amount of benefits due the patient, there is no doubt that there will be instances of controversy. In fact, Mr. President, it is often the case that the rules and regulations employed to administer such laws are perfected in the long run by the ability of beneficiaries to appeal adverse decisions.
>
> Mr. President, I have asked representatives of the Social Security Administration and other experts to explain the rationale for a $1,000 limitation on beneficiary appeals. The only explanation is one of concern over administrative caseloads as well as concern over the number of cases that may pile up in the courts. I have investigated all the other programs under our Social Security laws and have not found one instance where a beneficiary's right to appeal has been conditioned upon the amount in question. Under those titles of public assistance where administration is relegated to the States, I have found that in each instance it is stated in our laws that the Secretary will only approve a State plan if rights of appeal are provided for, regardless of the amount in question.
>
> I am opposed to any provision that places a burden on the elderly rather than on program administrators.
>
> 111 Cong. Rec. 1536 (1965) (remarks of Senator Kennedy).

In 1972, Congress amended the Medicare Act substantially, extending the limitations of hearings to Part B beneficiary claims in order to eliminate the expense and inconvenience of a formal hearing when the disputed amount was small. The Senate Finance Committee defended such action, saying:

> Experience under the program indicated that the holding of a full fair hearing is unwarranted in cases where the amount in controversy is relatively small. Carriers have reported cases involving $5 and $10 claims for which the cost of holding a fair hearing has exceeded $100.
>
> S. Rep. No. 1230, 92nd Cong., 2d Sess. 213 (1972).

At the time of the appellate court's decision in March of 1981, the law relating to Part A rights to a hearing in matters of disputes over claims remained limited to cases involving more than $100. Curiously enough, HHS tended to refer to the latter as a "paper hearing." The Gray Panthers objected not only to the inadequacies of such paper explanations, but also the unconstitutionality of that part of the law relating to denials of claims under $100.

In essence, the Gray Panthers lost their claim of unconstitutionality but gained some kind of victory in their claim that the paper explanations were inadequate. The appellate court's decision, however, posed a peculiar problem. HHS was enjoined to work out a better explanation form and the Gray Panthers were entitled to object to any continuing weaknesses and to offer their own suggestions for remedy.

The Original Form Sent to Beneficiaries

Before the appellate court's reversal, the form used by HHS in denying a beneficiary's claim was as follows (printed in large capital letters across the empty spaces in section number one were the words, THIS IS NOT A BILL), and the back side of the notice begins with "ALWAYS GIVE YOUR HEALTH INSURANCE CLAIM NUMBER . . . " (See Figure 1-1.)

Attached to this notice was a listing of service codes. The appropriate code numbers were placed in the box on the reverse side of the notice to explain to the beneficiary what was understood by HHS. See Figure 1-2.

In response to the appellate court's mandate to make the forms more readable and understandable to the beneficiaries, HHS offered only one substantive change to page one as shown in Figure 1-3.

Several other changes were made in the headings at the top of the page, involving placement of the date, health insurance number, and beneficiary's name. Added to the bottom of that page was a place to insert the name of a representative, if any, and a mysterious space called "Appendix to Affidavit."

On the reverse side of the notice revised by HHS to meet the court's requirements, we also find very few changes. Under "2. IF YOU NEED MORE INFORMATION," SSA's 800 telephone number appears. The wording of "3.TIME LIMIT FOR FILING CLAIMS," was shortened to: "When a person could not file his claim within these limits because of an error or delay of the Social Security Administration or of a Medicare carrier or intermediary, these limits do not apply." In "4. HOW MUCH DOES MEDICARE PAY," a question mark was added, along with another paragraph, as follows: "Medicare pays 100% of the reasonable charge for Physician services to live donors provided in connection with kidney donation to an entitled beneficiary."

The service code information was condensed and placed on the back side rather than as a separate sheet. "Nursing home" was added as number "8" to the place of service code and HHS finally decided to use alphabetic codes for type of service, rather than, as in the original, leaving open the possibility of either alphabetic or numeric codes.

_______ EXPLANATION OF MEDICARE BENEFITS

DATE:
YOUR MEDICARE NUMBER
HEALTH INS. CLAIM NO.

THIS IS A STATEMENT OF THE ACTION ON YOUR MEDICARE CLAIM
KEEP THIS NOTICE FOR YOUR RECORDS

Always use this number when writing about your claim

BENEFICIARY OR REPRESENTATIVE	BENEFITS PAID TO:

1. SERVICES WERE PROVIDED BY	2. WHEN	3. AMOUNT BILLED	4. AMOUNT APPROVED	5. EXPLANATION OF ANY DIFFERENCE	SERVICE CODE (see back)
	TOTALS				
				MEDICARE PAID	REMARKS
Inpatient radiology and pathology physician services and certain laboratories paid in full					
Amount payable at 80% after the annual deductible					
Amount applied toward annual deductible					You have met _____ of the deductible for
Balance payable at 80%				PLEASE BE SURE TO READ THE IMPORTANT INFORMATION ON THE BACK OF THIS NOTICE.	
TOTAL MEDICARE PAYMENT					

Use the Attached Request for Medicare Payment Form the Next Time You Wish to Claim Medicare Benefits

THIS IS YOUR CHECK DETACH ON DOTTED LINE

- -

Rev. 477

FIGURE 1-1. Explanation of Medicare Benefits Notice

ALWAYS GIVE YOUR HEALTH INSURANCE CLAIM NUMBER WHEN WRITING ABOUT YOUR CLAIM. BRING THIS NOTICE WITH YOU IF YOU INQUIRE AT A SOCIAL SECURITY OFFICE.

1. IMPORTANT-YOU CAN USE THIS NOTICE:
   a. To show your physician or supplier how much of the annual deductible you have met as of the date of this notice.
   b. As a record of bills paid or denied. (If you sent in other medical expenses not shown on this form, you will get a separate notice.)
   c. To collect other insurance. If you have other health insurance, you may use this notice to claim benefits from your private insurance policy. Since your private insurace company may keep this notice, you may wish to keep a record of this information or ask your insurance company for a photocopy.
2. IF YOU NEED MORE INFORMATION:
   a. Check your Medicare Handbook;
   b. Contact a Social Security Office; or
   c. Contact (carrier name, address, phone).
3. TIME LIMIT FOR FILING CLAIMS:

For Services Received	File Claims By
Oct. 1, 1970–Sept. 30, 1971	Dec. 31, 1972
Oct. 1, 1971–Sept. 30, 1972	Dec. 31, 1973
Oct. 1, 1972–Sept. 30, 1973	Dec. 31, 1974
Oct. 1, 1973–Sept. 30, 1974	Dec. 31, 1975

Where a person could not file his claim within these limits because of an error or delay of the Social Security Administration or of a Medicare carrier or intermediary, the time limit may be extended if the claim is filed within 6 months after the error is corrected.

4. HOW MUCH DOES MEDICARE PAY? Medicare pays 80% of the charges in Column 4 above the annual deductible. The annual deductable is now $60. For calendar years before 1973 it was $50. Medicare pays 100% of the charges in column 4 for radiology and pathology services from physician while you are a bed patient in a qualified hospital.
5. IF PAYMENT NOT BASED ON THE FULL AMOUNT BILLED
   The amount Medicare may pay under law is limited to the lowest of:
   a. Customary charge, i.e., the charge made by the physician or supplier in 50% of his billings during the base year.
   b. Prevailing charge, i.e., the charge made 75% of the time by other physicians or suppliers for similar services in the area during the base year.
6. YOUR RIGHT TO REVIEW THE CASE
   If you have a problem or questions about the way your claim was handled or about the amount paid, please get in touch with the carrier (name and address) within 6 months of the date of this notice.

   The Social Security Office will help you file a request for review of your claim if it is more convenient.

USE THIS SPACE TO SHOW PLACE AND TYPE OF SERVICE CODES

Rev. 391, 477

FIGURE 1-1. (continued)

The following is a key to the codes used for the place and type of service shown in the "See Reverse" column on the face of the EOMB.

Place of Service (entry to left)		*Type of Service* (entry to right)
1. Office		1. Medicare care
2. Home		2. Surgery (includes treatment of fractures)
3. Inpatient hospital		3. Consultation
4. Skilled Nursing Facility		4. Diagnostic X-ray
5. Outpatient hospital		5. Diagnostic laboratory
6. Independent laboratory		6. Radiation therapy
7. Other		7. Anesthesia
		8. Assistance at surgery
		9. Other medical service
	or	10. Whole blood and packed red blood cells

Place of Service (entry to left)	*Type of Service* (entry to right)
1. Office	A. Medical care
2. Home	B. Surgery (includes treatment of fractures)
3. Inpatient hospital	C. Consultation
4. Skilled Nursing Facility	D. Diagnostic X-ray
5. Outpatient hospital	E. Diagnostic laboratory
6. Independent laboratory	F. Radiation therapy
7. Other	G. Anesthesia
	H. Assistance at surgery
	I. Other medical service
	J. Whole blood and packed red blood cells

Rev. 346, 477

FIGURE 1-2. Medicare Service Code

2. WHEN				
FROM		TO		
MO.	DAY	MO.	DAY	YR.

FIGURE 1-3. HHS Changes in EOMB Notice

In their May 21, 1981 response brief to the court which accompanied these revisions, HHS's attorneys, Charles F.C. Ruff and Royce C. Lamberth, made the following observations by way of justifying the claim that HHS had therein met the court's requirements. Noting that 159,000,000 claims are submitted annually for adjudication or payment, about twenty five million are initially denied, two-thirds of which involve reasonable charges of physician's bills. They note that claimants seek reviews in more than two million claims denied, about half of which are ultimately allowed after the review. This staggering fact leads HHS to say:

> . . . claims at the initial level must necessarily be undertaken by computer systems using their mass capabilities and are not done by individuals (as presumed by the Court of Appeals). And at the review level, two million claims can only feasibly be processed in the nature of a paper hearing . . . this does not require that the claimant have direct oral communication with a decision maker.

With this information at the forefront, HHS goes on to point out the revisions toward clarity to the beneficiaries noted above, the addition of a toll-free number heading the list.

The Court of Appeals, in its reversal, had stated that HHS's current procedure was lacking in that it was "unsupplemented by any opportunity to **communicate personally**" (p. 42), that "opportunity for an **oral interview or consultation** could alleviate some of the problems caused by the inadequate notice" (p. 46), and "the chance to talk to someone in charge would at least offer the claimant the opportunity to discover the basis of his dispute with the agency, and, if he has a defense, either answer on the spot or prepare rebuttal material for later submission" (p. 46).

At this point in the dispute, the National Senior Citizens Law Center called me and requested my linguistic assistance. There seemed to be two issues to address: (1) Can this or any other paper hearing approach be fixed in such a way that beneficiaries can understand the basis of the denial of their claims, understand the appeal remedies, get help from other knowledgeable resources, learn how to submit additional evidence regarding their claims? and, (2) Can a telephone call seeking such remedies be enough to satisfy the due process requirements outlined by law? Here we will deal only with the first issue, leaving the telephonic alternative for a later chapter.

I produced two reports to the Gray Panthers: the first dealt with communication problems inherent in the original HHS Explanation of Medicare Benefits form and the second was an analysis of the HHS revision of that form produced in response to the appellate court's demand that the form be revised in such a way that each claimant would be given a precise explanation as to why the claim was denied.

Problems with the Original Explanation of Medicare Benefits

This form is couched in a language code that is specific to the medical profession and not necessarily clear to outsiders to that profession. To make matters even worse, however, the form is also couched in a language code of business that is also not particularly clear to outsiders to that field of expertise. The special vocabulary, knowledge base or schema, punctuation system, and abbreviation conventions are not easily predictable to the average Medicare beneficiary. The use of such a restricted code puts the beneficiary at a distinct disadvantage, not only in understanding what the specialists in medicine and business intend, but also in being able to determine what sort of evidence they might put together to support their claims.

Many problems can be seen in the current form: the use of medical jargon, accounting jargon, ungrammaticality, unnecessary substitution of code numbers for words that might explain what the service was for, document design, and lack of recipient perspective.

The first page, column 5, reads, "EXPLANATION OF ANY DIFFERENCE BETWEEN COLUMNS 3 & 4, MEDICARE DOES NOT PAY FOR:" This is, to say the least, confusing. The difference between the amount billed (column 3) and the amount approved (column 4) is clear enough. One can assume that HHS intended column 5 to be a space for an explanation of why they were not going to pay any difference that might be there. This also assumes that comprehendable explanations for such facts can be reduced to the few lines permitted by this form. The capitalized heading for column 5, however, is ungrammatical as it now stands. The comma is a key problem, since it seems to separate what might well be two separate sentences. In Judge Wald's appellate court opinion, this comma is omitted, suggesting that even he did not comprehend the thrust of the column 5 heading. Another form distributed by HHS, but not described in full here, called "EXPLANATION OF NONCOVERED SERVICES," also deletes the comma as it refers to the caption of column 5, suggesting either that HHS is also confused by the meaning of this caption or that it is impervious to its possible confusion.

The form is heavy with nominalizations, such as "Inpatient radiology and pathology physician services," and "HEALTH INSURANCE CLAIM NUMBER." When entire sentences are used, it tends to prefer syntax with beginning dependent clauses, such as: "If you have other health insurance, you may use this notice to claim benefits from your private insurance policy," and the odd sentence, "Where a person could not file his claim within these limits because of an error or delay of the Social Security Administration or of a Medicare carrier or intermediary, the time limit may be extended if the claim is filed within 6 months after the error is corrected." In clear administrative writing, of course, the main part of the sentence should be fronted, not deferred by one or more subordinate clauses.

Medical and accounting terms of art, or jargon, include: "Inpatient radiology and pathology physician services," "Amount payable at 80% after the annual deductible," "Balance payable," "Customary charge," "Prevailing charge," "SERVICE CODES," and "REVIEW OF THE CASE." Some beneficiaries may understand some or all of these terms but there is no reason to take that chance if other, more user-friendly terms could replace them.

Print type and capitalization also contribute to reader confusion here. This form contains many different print sizes and type. It is a recognized principle of readability that although mixed print type can be used effectively, it should be done so with great care and planning. One principle is that like items should have the same print type. Another principle is that the larger or bolder the type, the more important the message. It is difficult to imagine that the most important message on this form is that it is not a bill. Application of the users' perspective would dictate that the most important information would be the amount of the total payment to them (see chapter 2 on the training program at SSA).

It is also a well recognized principle in readability that long statements written in all capital letters are harder to read, and therefore harder to comprehend, than sentences written in conventional, predictable orthography containing grammatically acceptable upper and lower case letters. The sentence at the bottom right hand of the first page of the form,

> PLEASE BE SURE TO READ THE
> IMPORTANT INFORMATION ON
> THE BACK SIDE OF THIS NOTICE

although important to both the beneficiary and to Medicare, is unnecessarily difficult in this regard. Readers may be accustomed to reading one whole line of all capital letters in newspaper headlines, but not three. I am reminded of the experience I had in the home of a U.S. senator a few years ago. After lunch, while waiting for the Superbowl game to come on television, he was reviewing an important speech he was about to give but was stumbling with the text and making error after error. When I asked to look at his script, I discovered that it was printed in all capital letters. I suggested that he have it retyped in conventional orthography but with larger type. He did so and presented his speech in his usual flawless manner. Like most people, he was unaware of the readability problem posed by all capital letters.

A variation of the problem posed by all capital letters is the one posed by capitalizing each content word in a sentence, contrary to conventional writing practice in English. Near the bottom of the first page of this notice, the following sentence appears: "Use the Attached Request for Medicare Payment Form Next Time You Wish to Claim Medicare Benefits." Capital letters are used for all except the function words, "the," "for," "to." Most of us are at least slowed down by such practice.

Although when I came into this dispute it had already been determined that this original form was unacceptable, and that my major assignment was to address the revision that HHS was mandated to create, I offered my suggestions to the Gray Panthers for revising this form as an anchor against the forthcoming revisions that HHS was to make. I noted the following potential changes in page one of this notice:

1. Use words, not code numbers, to describe what the service was for. It would also be useful for this column to be next to column 1, the service provider.
2. Add a subject and a verb to column 3, changing "AMOUNT BILLED" to "Amount you were billed."
3. Have column 4 read, "Amount we approve."
4. Split column 5 into two things: (1) "Explanation of any difference between columns 3 and 4" and, separately, (2) "Medicare does not pay for the following."
5. Revise box marked "MEDICARE PAID" to "Paid by Medicare."
6. Change "Inpatient radiology and pathology physician services and certain laboratories paid in full" to "the full amount of charges for radiology, physicians doing pathology, and laboratory costs."
7. Revise "Amount payable at 80% after the annual deductible" to "We will pay 80% of this after you have first paid your annual deductible of $100." The original wording assumes that the beneficiaries know that there is an annual deduction, that they know what that amount is, that they know when "annual" begins (January 1, fiscal year, or time the policy was started?).
8. Change "Amount applied toward annual deductible" to "Before we can pay you, you must have paid the first $100 in each year. If you have not yet paid this amount, we deduct this amount from this payment."
9. Delete "Balance payable at 80%" since it is collapsed into the following box (paragraph 10 below). In any case, "payable" does not specify who is paying and who is getting paid.
10. Revise "TOTAL MEDICARE PAYMENT" to "Medicare pays 80% of this amount." The original wording is ambiguous as to who is paying whom. Readers could understand it to mean either the amount payable to them (apparently the intended meaning) or the amount they must pay for services.
11. Change "THIS IS YOUR CHECK" to "Below is your check."

HHS's Response to the Court Order to Revise the Form

My task, to this point, was not to revise the form for HHS but, rather, only to offer suggestions about how they might do so. When their plan for revision was made available, I noticed a few effective changes. For example, page two of the form revised by HHS contained reasonably clear phrasing and vocabulary. But one thing remaining clear about the page was that it had no real title or focus. It listed six numbered items that contained useful information, but with no particular organizing scheme. As I analyzed it, the form appeared to contain three suggestions to beneficiaries about what they could do about the relatively unchanged page one of that form. It also added answers to six unexpressed questions that claimants supposedly ask. I suggested, therefore, that the form be recast along this unexpressed but inherent organization. I also suggested that the questions that this page answers be recast to match the recipient's perspective. That is, they should be questions that the recipients ask, from their perspective, using personal pronouns such as "I" and "my." A draft of my suggested revision is as follows:

Suggestions:

- Always give your health insurance claim number when you write us about your claim. If you go to a Social Security office to ask about your claim, always bring this form with you.
- Use this form to show your physician or supplier how much of the yearly deductible you have paid as of the date of this form.
- Save this form as your personal record of bills paid or denied by Medicare. If you have sent in other medical expenses not shown on this form, we will send you a separate form to fill out and send back to us.

Commonly Asked Questions:

Question: How can I make claims to other insurance companies that also insure me?

Answer: If you have other health insurance policies, you can use this form to claim the benefits from those companies. Since your private insurance company may decide to keep this form, you should keep a record of this information or ask your private insurance company for a photocopy of it.

Question: How can I find more information about my Medicare policy?

Answer: First, look for the information you need in the Medicare Handbook which you received when you subscribed to Medicare. If you still do not find what you need to know, telephone or visit your local Social Security office or your private insurance company.

Question: When must I file my claims?

Answer: Any claims made between October 1, 1980 and September 30, 1981 must be filed by December 31, 1981. If you cannot file your claim within these limits because of an error or delay of the Social Security Administration or of a Medicare carrier or intermediary, the time limit may be extended as long as the claim is filed within six months after this error or delay is corrected.

Question: How much does Medicare pay?

Answer: Medicare pays 80% of the charges in column 4 after the $100 yearly deductible has been subtracted from the total amount of your first annual claim. Medicare pays 100% of the charges in column 4 for radiology and pathology services by physicians during the time you are a bed patient in a qualified hospital.

Question: Why was my payment not for the full amount of my claim?

Answer: The amount that Medicare can pay you is limited by law to whichever of the following is the lowest amount of money:

1. The customary charges made by a physician or supplier for 50% of the billings he makes during the year. This was used as a base for his customary charge.
2. The prevailing charge made 75% of the time by other physicians or suppliers for the same or similar services in your local area during the year that was used as a base for this comparison.

Question: How can I appeal my case?

Answer: If you have a problem about the way your claim was handled or about the amount paid, please telephone or write the

> carrier within six months of the date on this form. The Social Security office will help you file a request for a review of your claim if this is more convenient for you.

Therefore, some two months after the appellate court asked HHS to revise this form to make it more readable and comprehensible to beneficiaries, HHS offered these changes. In effect, there was very little revision accomplished and few improvements made. My second report to the Gray Panthers was an analysis of the May 21, 1981 response and suggested revisions made by HHS and presented to the appellate court.

Further Suggestions for Revision

In this analysis to the Gray Panthers of HHS's suggested revisions, I noted the failure of HHS to improve the form along the lines I had originally outlined. Of course, these suggestions were not given to HHS until they had fulfilled their first requirement. As much as anything else, I wanted all parties involved to begin to understand the ramifications of substituting a paper hearing, even one supplemented by a possible telephonic episode, when seen in light of actual face-to-face interaction. For this reason, my report dealt in large part with the problems inherent with a paper hearing.

Problems with a Paper Hearing

The proposal submitted by HHS in response to the decision of the Court of Appeals maintains an HHS perspective rather than a beneficiary perspective.

By perspective, I refer to what also might be called "point of view." The areas of public service, at whatever level the bureaucracy might be, were conceived with the idea that the public's perspective is to be considered foremost. The basic question is (or should be), "what does the public want?" If the public wants something that is not possible to obtain, it needs to be told this. But if the public desire is within the bounds of the bureaucracy to provide and is supported by law, it should be possible for that government to enable the public to get it. In fact, it is imperative that the government help the public receive it.

In the case in point, the public is entitled to certain rights concerning medical insurance. The perspective of the consumer should cause the bureaucracy to see to it that the true rights of the public are realized and delivered, that misunderstood rights are clarified, and that falsely presumed rights are corrected and denied. It cannot be expected that consumers can immediately understand the bureaucracy's point of view. The agency is the specialist in this area. The public consists of amateurs who use the service infrequently and are not up to speed on all the variables involved. Just as it behooves a teacher to try to understand the beginning points of the learner, so it is incumbent upon the agency, the specialist, to try to see issues from the point of view of the amateur beneficiary. This is not to say that the agency should bend rules or falsify; rather, it means that the agency, as public servant, should do its best to see what the public's perspective is and to adjust its comments and explanations to that perspective.

Paper hearings, by definition, ignore the consumer's perspective because there is no point at which the public can express or initiate that perspective. The beneficiaries in this case can only respond to the bureaucracy's perspective. In a sense, their language rights are denied. The paper hearing is a one-way communication from agency to beneficiary, with no interaction and, therefore, no possibility of discovering the beneficiary's topics or perspectives. To determine perspective, there must be interaction which permits the beneficiaries to present their perspectives, not just to respond to the perspectives of the agency. In short, one cannot express a point of view if the structure of the communication excludes the possibility of it happening. The structure of communication now in effect in the paper hearing is as follows:

Agency	*Claimant*
Asks information questions (through application form)	Responds by reporting facts (by filling out form)
Evaluates claimant's response (through EOMB form)	

To this point, the claimant has engaged in only one type of communicative activity, that of responding to the questions of the agency. The agency sets the agenda and evaluates the claimant's response, much as a classroom teacher asks a question, then assigns a grade to the answer. That answer, amazingly enough, is then taken as an indication of what the student knows, even though that student may know a great deal about matters that were never asked.

It is clear that if the claimants have a communication agenda, there has been no place, in this structure, to produce it. Therefore, it is never known by the agency. To be truly responsive to the claimant's perspective, it is necessary to permit them a communicative "turn." This can happen only if the claimants get an opportunity to initiate a topic, or begin a turn of talk, as round two in the communicative exchange, as follows:

Claimant	*Agency*
Describes view of the issue, requests information, procedures, or clarifications (through oral hearing)	Responds to claimant by reporting facts (through oral hearing)

Since it is not the role of the claimants to evaluate the agency's response, the only appropriate further interaction is to continue to explain, clarify, and/or request information, which would amount to further rounds of communicative interaction. Since it cannot be predicted what will be unknown, misunderstood, or unclear to the claimants, there is no feasible way to substitute a paper hearing for what is most humanly efficient as oral communication.

If the paper hearing is inadequate for obtaining the beneficiaries' perspectives, this is not because of any inability on the part of the claimants, nor is it necessarily attributable to any ill will of the agency. The fault lies in the communicative structure necessitated by the use of paper forms to negotiate resolution. Forms ask only what the agency wants or needs to know, not what the claimants know or want to know. Questions are interpretable in many ways, no matter how clear they may seem to their originators. Extenuating circumstances, misunderstandings, gaps in memory, and vagueness all contribute to this. Paper hearings lack the continuous dialogue found in oral conversation, that which enables human beings to build up their understanding, piece by piece, as new information is acquired. The paper hearing puts all its thrust only on one conversational turn.

Failure to Capture Beneficiaries' Perspective

Further evidence of the failure of HHS to see the beneficiaries' perspective can be found in its response to the court's order for revision (Defendant's Proposed Plan, 1981). The attorneys for HHS refer to the claimants' need for "better understanding of the denial of their claims" (p. 2). Claimants need considerably more understanding than why their claims were denied. What about the claimants' need for more information? What about the claimants' possible belief that the agency had made an error or overlooked important facts? In that circumstance HHS seemed to have a myopic view of the communicative event. It was certainly not one that captured the beneficiaries' point of view. The HHS response continues this thought on the following page, offering that personnel "will respond to the claimant's questions by further explaining why his claim was denied" (p. 3). The interesting assumption here is that claimants want a hearing because they do not understand why they are at fault.

In addition to needing to know why their claims were denied, HHS admits that claimants may want more information about what the Medicare requirements are, what the appeal rights are, and to gain specific information about their claims. These are, indeed, issues about which the claimants may need further information, but they are not the only issues. The agency's response makes no provision for the possibility that the claimant may have something to tell Medicare, and may wish not to just ask them questions. Effective communication is predicated on the possibility of both parties being able to report what they consider to be relevant information, to clarify or seek clarification of information already exchanged, and to request further information or probe more deeply.

Futility of Follow-up Telephone Communication

The toll free telephone approach suggested by HHS is inadequate on several grounds. To begin with, HHS assumes that the major, if not sole purpose of the claimant's communication, is to request explanation for a claim denial. If they're wrong, claimants want to know why. Conversely, the role of Medicare, being right, is to explain why the claimant is wrong, what the rules are, and what their rights are in light of all this. This is what the paper hearing currently does. Nothing is added by the telephonic approach suggested here. The claimant is not expected to report new facts. Medicare reports facts to the claimant. We will delve more deeply into the controversy over telephonic hearings vs. face-to-face hearings in Chapter 2.

Resolution of the Case

In the end, the dispute between HHS and the Gray Panthers over the Explanation of Medicare Benefits form was resolved, as is most litigation, with compromises on both sides. HHS accepted many, but not all, of my suggestions, and it can be said that the result was at least an improvement, if not totally adequate. I seriously doubt that my arguments about taking the beneficiary's perspective were fully understood or even appreciated. Page one of the form, with all its bureaucratic faults, continued to be used in somewhat the same way, with some wording improvements. Page two was revised in pretty much the question-answer framework that I had suggested. I took some solace in the fact that the agency had managed to incorporate what I said about beneficiary perspective, although probably without fully understanding what it meant. They liked the looks of it, though not for the reasons I advocated.

It has been almost two decades since this issue was presented to me and it is not possible to keep up with the changes in forms and procedures that have taken place since. I have no up-to-date knowledge of what HHS is currently doing about the explanation of Medicare benefits. But this is the nature of this type of work. Hot issues are soon forgotten and new ones take their place. I present this chapter as an example of the intricate and complex workings of one effort to unravel a linguistic problem in a bureaucracy.

Chapter 2

Training a Bureaucracy to Write Clearly: A Case Study of the Social Security Administration

My past relationship with the National Senior Citizens Law Center (Gray Panthers) paved the way for a more recent case they brought against the U. S. Department of Health and Human Services (Gray Panthers v. Schweiker, Civil Action No. 77-488). The complaint was essentially that the Medicare report forms, issued to recipients by the Health Care Financing Administration, were unclear, if not unreadable. The Gray Panthers prevailed in court. HHS appealed the decision, but the appellate court supported the lower court's earlier decision. Finally, the case was put on appeal to the U. S. Supreme Court, which once again ruled for the plaintiff. As is often the case, even then the matter was not settled, since months of interpretation of various aspects of the decision had to be resolved. During this period, some eight years, Medicare recipients were limited in their receipt of services resulting from the court decision until the final agreements on these interpretations could be resolved.

Congress Mandates the Social Security Administration to Notify Beneficiaries about Supplemental Security Income

It should be pointed out that the above scenario of delay is one reason why the National Senior Citizens Law Center (NSCLC) is not predisposed to litigation. Even victories, such as this one, can be drawn out for an unconscionable amount of time. The most efficient way to get amicable resolution, they reason, is to seek agreement out of court. Therefore, when Congress required the Social Security Administration (SSA) to send a letter to all Social Security recipients, advising them they they might be eligible for additional benefits that they had hitherto not requested, the Gray Panthers wanted to resolve the matter peacefully. But when they were shown SSA's proposed letter, they came close to going back to court once again. The letter is reproduced here in full, preserving all its features (see Figure 2-1).

SSA's Original Effort to Comply with this Mandate

YOU MAY BE ABLE TO GET MONEY UNDER THIS SUPPLEMENTAL SECURITY INCOME (SSI) PROGRAM.

SSI IS A PROGRAM THAT PAYS MONTHLY CHECKS TO AGED, BLIND, OR DISABLED PEOPLE WHO DO NOT OWN MUCH AND HAVE LITTLE INCOME. SSI IS RUN BY THE SOCIAL SECURITY ADMINISTRATION, BUT IT IS NOT THE SAME AS SOCIAL SECURITY. SOME PEOPLE CAN RECEIVE MONEY FROM BOTH SSI AND SOCIAL SECURITY.

ARE THE THINGS YOU OWN (OTHER THAN YOUR HOME, CAR, INSURANCE POLICIES, BURIAL PLOTS, AND BURIAL FUNDS) WORTH $1,500 OR LESS (OR $2,500 OR LESS IF YOU ARE MARRIED AND LIVING WITH YOUR SPOUSE?

DO YOU GET LESS THAN $334.00 A MONTH IN INCOME FROM ALL SOURCES? IF YOU ARE MARRIED AND LIVING WITH YOUR SPOUSE, DO YOU AND YOUR SPOUSE RECEIVE LESS THAN $492.00 A MONTH? (INCOME MEANS CASH AND CHECKS YOU RECEIVE SUCH AS YOUR SOCIAL SECURITY CHECK, EARNINGS, PENSIONS, OR ANNUITIES. IT CAN ALSO MEAN ITEMS YOU RECEIVE FROM OTHERS, SUCH AS FOOD AND SHELTER.)

ARE YOU A CITIZEN OF THE UNITED STATES OR ARE YOU A LEGALLY ADMITTED ALIEN?

IF YOU CAN ANSWER YES TO THESE QUESTIONS, YOU MAY STILL BE ABLE TO GET SSI.

IF YOU THINK YOU MIGHT BE ABLE TO GET SSI, OR YOU ARE NOT SURE, PHONE OR VISIT ANY SOCIAL SECURITY OFFICE RIGHT AWAY. SSI PAYMENTS CAN START ONLY WITH THE DAY YOU FILE AN APPLICATION, OR THE DAY YOU MEET ALL THE REQUIREMENTS, WHICHEVER IS LATER. THE PEOPLE AT THE SOCIAL SECURITY OFFICE WILL TELL YOU HOW TO APPLY. THE PHONE NUMBER AND ADDRESS OF THE SOCIAL SECURITY OFFICE ARE LISTED IN YOUR PHONE BOOK UNDER "SOCIAL SECURITY ADMINISTRATION."

FIGURE 2-1. SSA's Original Effort to Comply with Mandate

Revision of SSA's Attempt to Comply with This Mandate

The Gray Panthers' problem was immediately apparent. In order to really help the SSA here it would be necessary to rewrite this letter for them. That's when they called on me to draft an alternate version that would be clearer and more effective. I submitted the following draft to the Gray Panthers:

IS YOUR SOCIAL SECURITY ENOUGH TO LIVE ON?
IF NOT,
YOU MAY BE ABLE TO GET MORE MONEY

The following are six questions that people like you often ask, along with our answers to help you.

How can I get more money from Social Security?

If you are over 65, disabled, or blind, you may be able to get more benefits from the Supplemental Security Income program, called SSI. It's not the same as your Social Security benefits but we run both programs. We set up SSI to give additional benefits to those who are over 65, disabled, or blind.

How can I get these additional benefits?

It depends on what you own and how much it is worth. To figure this out, we don't count any of the following things you might own:

- your home
- your car
- your burial plot or burial insurance
- your furniture and belongings up to $2,000 worth
- $1,500 in any other money or things you own (If you are married and living with your spouse, this amount is $2,250.)

But we do count the following things:

- the amount of your Social Security check
- any salary, pension, or other money you get
- the costs of housing and food if these are paid for by someone else

Then we add these together and see how much you get now and how much more money you are entitled to under our SSI program.

Well, how much more money can I get?

We add up your current income and if it comes to less than $334 each month now, we will give you more money (up to $334) in SSI benefits. If you are married and living with your spouse, you can get up to $492 each month with extra SSI benefits. You may also be able to get up to $______month from the state where you live. If you are married this figure comes to $______a month.

But what about additional medical costs?

If you get **any** money at all from SSI, even a few dollars, many states will give you Medicaid money. This will help pay your medical bills that are not paid by Medicare. So it is very important for you to be getting even small amounts of SSI money.

How can I find out more about this?

- Come to our office, if you can. We'll be glad to help you, or
- Call us on the telephone. We are listed in your telephone book under Social Security Administration. You can also get our telephone number by dialing 411.

If I get more money from SSI will my regular Social Security check be different?

No. We just want you to know what extra money you might be able to get. Your Social Security check will stay the same. Any extra money will be from SSI.

By the way, if you already get SSI money, you are probably getting everything that is available to you. But if you are in doubt, call us. If you don't get SSI money now and if you think you are eligible for it, we invite you to apply. But we can't pay you more money unless you tell us.

Sincerely,

Your Social Security Administration

When I submitted this draft to the Gray Panthers, I accompanied it with a letter to its then director, Eileen P. Sweeney. Exerpts of this letter try to explain what it is that I did to the original SSA notice, as follows:

> . . . NSCLC will probably have a greater effect on agencies such as SSA if you take the stance of helping them rather than fighting them. For one thing, government agencies are often accused of being impersonal and uncaring. Perhaps this is true but I doubt that they want to be . . . What I've tried to do here is to work on the premise that the SSA cares about the real problems of real people. If they don't let that disposition be shown, we will help them with it.
>
> . . . What is at the heart of being personal? Clearly it is dialogue, one-on-one communication between one human being and another. For this reason, I have designed the form in the shape of a dialogue, a conversation that might occur if an SSA person met a senior citizen. In my opinion, the senior citizen who reads this ought to feel more involved, more cared about and clearer than he/she would be if given a bureaucratic announcement.
>
> . . . Note also that the SSA version announces a benefit but still gives the impression that the senior citizen is too dumb to figure it out. We need to assume comprehension in the way we say things if we expect to get it. Our task is to be so clear that the seniors understand well enough not to have to bother the SSA offices further. It is a matter of tone as well as clarity. . . . A nice touch to these questions and answers that would make the notice more caring and personal would be for the commissioner to actually sign it, like a normal letter. . . . In terms of document design, I would use all caps very sparingly. Perhaps the only place would be in the first three lines. Most people are used to all caps only in headlines of newspapers. If not all caps, I would use large boldface print for these three lines. The six questions and answers should be set off in bold face non-caps and not indented . . . I would use bullets where lists occur, especially if the information is crucial.

The Gray Panthers liked my revision and submitted it to SSA as a reasonable alternative. They also pointed out some technical errors in the SSA original version (which explains differences between money amounts in the two versions above) along with noting that it would be extremely helpful if the notice were also to include state supplemental benefit levels.

SSA's Request That We Train Their Notice-Writing Staff

Not only did the Gray Panthers like my revision, SSA almost immediately agreed with it as well, proving my hypothesis that the bureaucracy did not intend to camouflage the information; they were only weak in expressing it. To my utter surprise, a few weeks after this matter was happily resolved, I received a phone call from the office of Martha McSteen, then acting commissioner of SSA at its Baltimore headquarters. She complimented me on my work and asked me if I could come to Baltimore and help with SSA's newly created "Clear Writing Staff" to improve SSA's notice-writing, one of the eight priorities the agency had recently established. It seems that SSA was quite aware of the inadequacies of their letters (which SSA refers to as "notices"). My first reaction was to check with the National Senior Citizens Law Center to see if they had any objections, since the two organizations had done battle so many times before. Switching sides might not seem appropriate. Eileen Sweeney was absolutely delighted by McSteen's request and gave me an immediate go-ahead to accept the assignment.

Preparations by SSA

Using considerable wisdom, acting commissioner McSteen decided upon a project management approach for solving the notice-writing problems which had plagued the agency in the past. Essentially, this approach featured certain elements critical to solving these problems. Toward this end, McSteen ordered that:

1. One of the four deputy commissioners of SSA be designated to oversee the activities required to reach a solution. She named Herbert R. Doggett, Jr., SSA's deputy commissioner for operations, as the executive manager for the project on clear notice-writing.
2. Periodic progress reports be given directly to her. Initially, the acting commissioner and her deputies received, on a monthly basis, both a written and an oral report. This stringent requirement allowed problems to be detected and solved quickly at the agency's highest decision-making level.
3. A project management team be established. Each of the four deputy commissioners and SSA's assistant general counsel named high-level managers to serve on the team. By this strategy, all of the agency's concerns about notices were represented on the team. Doggett named Barbara Schnackenberg as his project director. She devoted her attention to managing both the project team and the newly created notice-writing staff.

This last point on the project management approach was especially crucial since, from the outset, it permitted the concerns of the four divisions of the agency and the General Counsel to be clearly delineated. The project was, in a very real sense, one of language planning and, as is typical in language planning issues, the perceptions of the community must first be made very clear if the planning is to be successful. From an early discussion, members of the Policy, Systems, Management, and Operations divisions clarified that they had somewhat different perceptions of their goals.

The Policy people wanted to be certain that, whatever writing changes came about, no variations from the regulations and SSA policy would occur. The Systems people wanted to be sure that notices could be generated by SSA's computers or through other word processing capabilities. At that time, the computers at SSA were already nearly outmoded and taxed to capacity. The Management people wanted to be certain that project activities were funded, that any needed procurements were properly obtained, that any needed training would be delivered correctly, and that the project would solve the problems that were identified through notice-quality reviews. It should be pointed out that the agency had been receiving many critical letters from recipients, families, and friends of SSA beneficiaries about the unclear, confusing, and outwardly inaccurate notices sent to them. Some such letters, in fact, had even come from members of Congress. The Operations people wanted to be sure that notices clearly conveyed the proper message. The frustration of the public had resulted in such a high volume of inquiries and complaints that their field facilities were being heavily taxed. The General counsel's office, while not technically a part of SSA's organization, was nevertheless charged with defending notices in possible court cases and wanted to be sure that the intent of the law was carried out.

After considering the dimensions of the problem and the nature of the prospective task, I suggested to SSA that it would take two people to conduct such training, both a linguist and a psychologist. And I knew the perfect psychologist, Dr. Jana Staton, who had also done research on writing. Since she is my wife, our teamwork would be made easier. Ms. McSteen agreed, and we went to the main office of SSA to get an orientation and make some initial ethnographic observations.

Early Ethnographic Observations

Our informal discussions with the SSA clear-writing team were very informative. They were somewhat frustrated, felt under seige, and believed that they were powerless. One writer expressed that no matter what he wrote, it would be changed either by the General Counsel's office, by the Policy office, or by the limitations of the computer. Others agreed.

Like most job reassignments in bureaucracies, the clear-writing team had been assembled from many different branches of SSA. Those who came from Systems knew what the limitations of the computer system were. In the mid-eighties, computer technology was rapidly changing. Ironically, SSA had recently completed a new building that was designed to contain the old main frame computers, but the developing technology of microcomputers had made much of that new building unnecessary. Still, again like most bureaucracies, change comes only with great difficulty and effort and SSA's outmoded computer system was still limping along.

There was also a strong undercurrent, noted from our early observations and discussions with the clear writing team, that the final say in what went into their writing was dictated by the General Counsel's office. Somehow, fear had been struck into their hearts that they might write something that the lawyers disagreed with or which actually misstated the law and regulations.

In short, our early observations pointed out to us that the writers felt that they had no authority, that they were low persons in the pecking order, and that they were the ones that got all the blame as the criticisms poured in. To say the least, morale was not high as McSteen's new priority began. But the acting commissioner had sewn good seeds when she brought the five SSA areas together on one team. It opened the door for a common communication capability within the agency, at least at the management level, which had not previously existed for notice-writing.

Noting this intra-agency management approach, Staton and I decided that it also would be a good thing to include representatives from Policy, Systems, and the General Counsel's office in any actual training programs that we might design. If communication across departments is a good thing at the management level, wouldn't it be equally good at the actual writing level? Wouldn't the low persons in the pecking order be empowered by the presence of the perceived authorities in this venture? The possible danger, of course, was that this idea might backfire and the presumed powerful segments of SSA might intimidate the writers even more. To guard against this problem, Staton and I interviewed various representatives of the Systems, Policy, and General Counsel divisions about this feared asymmetry of power. Our findings confirmed the notion that the idea was a good one. Systems was not afraid of our being critical of their old fashioned computers. In fact, they seemed to welcome such criticism since it would strengthen their case for upgrading their entire system. Policy felt no conflict and, in fact, welcomed the possibility that analysis of the regulations might make them clearer to even that office. The General Counsel's office, contrary to the belief of the writing team, did not feel that the terms of art and legal jargon of the law had to be replicated in every notice that the agency sent out.

Our findings about the real attitudes of the various pieces of the puzzle were encouraging, but we worried that such information might remain only at the management level. We asked, therefore, that at least one representative of the General Counsel's office, Systems, and Policy be included as actual workshop participants. In this way, the notice-writers could hear with their own ears what we heard as we talked with the management level of these areas. Incidentally, it also gave us the opportunity to see whether or not management level beliefs were, in fact, broadly shared by their divisions. As it turns out, they were. Having attorneys, computer people, and policy types in the workshops did exactly what we had hoped. It gave the writers assurance that their fears about writing notices inappropriate to the law that might exceed their computer capabilities or be contrary to policy could be overcome.

Designing the Training Program

Staton and I next set about to design a training program that would be both psychologically and linguistically sound as well as helpful to the agency. But one more step still had to be taken. SSA has a division of training programs that oversees all internal and external training of SSA employees. When we met with the director of training programs, we learned that it was customary for such programs to be what was called "off the shelf programs." That is, outside training vendors were to present to the office of training a complete syllabus of the proposed program for evaluation and approval before the training could begin. Other vendors had provided training in English grammar and other somewhat related topics in the past and the director wanted to see what our "off the shelf" program was like. The problem was that we did not plan to make use of this type of training approach. To use their jargon, we had nothing "in the can."

Instead of bringing our theory and knowledge to the writers, we wanted to have them bring their writing issues to us. We would then create the teaching out of the real, daily issues encountered by the notice-writers. We could guess at what these problems might be, but we felt that it would be more efficient to let the participants direct the training to more local issues. This was hard to explain and even harder to get accepted. The acting commissioner understood what we meant, however, and she intervened with the director of training to let us give our way a try. This meant, of course, that the training director had to okay a program that he had not seen and assessed, sidestepping the bureaucracy that had been in place for years. Perhaps reluctantly, he did so, and the first bureaucratic hurdle had been overcome.

Having our method of training accepted, the next step was to consider the time and resource constraints of the agency, to say nothing of our own. After much discussion, the following plan was developed. No more than fifteen participants would be involved in any given training program. The hands-on approach we were taking would not permit a large number of participants, since each one would, in theory at least, bring his or her current writing problems to us for analysis and teaching. The lecture approach, common in SSA training, was not possible, thus limiting the workshop size to a manageable few. Staton and I are strong advocates of maturation time, so we asked that the program be spread out over at least six weeks, meeting for three hours once each week. This was met with a sigh of relief, since it took away only one morning a week from the participants' work schedule. We also argued that the participants would be expected to do outside-of-class "homework," including observation and interviewing as well as reading. This once a week schedule permitted the participants to bring in their current writing problems one week and have them analyzed the following week. It also gave Staton and me the chance to review and analyze these notices as well as to construct whatever teaching grew out of them as the following week's lesson.

The Training Program

With considerable trepidation, we conducted our first six-week workshop and anxiously awaited the evaluations of our students. The results were immediate and very positive. The writing project director asked for another round of workshops. In all, six sections of fifteen SSA participants were trained over a two-year period. During the second year of the training, it began to worry us that SSA might ask us to do such training in perpetuity. Discussing this fear with the director, we hit upon a way to make SSA more self sufficient in this regard. During the fifth training session, we picked four of our top students from the preceding four sessions to "intern" with us as we carried out this session. They were to plan with us and contribute whenever possible to the in-class discussions, with the idea that in the sixth session, our roles would be reversed. The interns would then do the major teaching and discussion while Staton and I would be on the sidelines, offering comments, but not being in charge. We thought of this as analagous to "practice teaching" in the field of education. We also considered this a way to empower the bureaucracy to become self sufficient. Our plan was followed and the four SSA employees we picked did an excellent job. We ended our association with SSA feeling that not only had we moved the field along, but that we also had provided some assurance that our work might continue after we were gone.

Features of the Training Program

We now turn our attention to the training program itself. Perhaps it is somewhat unfair to exhibit the sort of writing that exemplified the problems we faced as we conducted our training. It also should be pointed out that when millions of letters are sent out each year by this agency, a computerized approach was deemed necessary. Thus, the computer stored thousands of ready-made paragraphs in various letter categories such as award notices, denial notices, and so forth. When a letter was constructed, the computer was asked to assemble a series of paragraphs appropriate for that letter. Needless to say, the results were often disorganized and, occasionally, almost comical. In addition to writing by this method of selecting computer-stored paragraphs, SSA writers also often had to compose original letters on specific topics or blend their new paragraphs with computer-stored ones. SSA's overall task, then, concerned rewriting the body of thousands of extant paragraphs in the computer while, at the same time, improving the quality of their newly composed paragraphs. Also, a task that loomed large was to determine a method of making these individual paragraphs, whatever their origins, appear to be connected within the final notice product. It goes without saying that the notices also had to be accurate, clear, and understandable, at the same time presenting a proper, favorable, and positive impression of the agency and a sympathetic and non-condescending attitude toward the recipients.

One of the first notices that was brought to our attention by the participants was in frequent use at least until 1984, as reproduced in Figure 2-2.

Fieldwork

As homework, we asked the participants to find some actual SSA recipients and to interview them, sentence by sentence, about what they understood or misunderstood, liked or disliked, about this notice. The results were not surprising. Recipients were confused about its meaning and unclear about what they should do about the notice. The sequence of the letter was odd and few interviewed even recognized that the letter was actually an award notification, despite the fact that the large print at the top describes it as such.

Social Security
Award Certificate

From: Department of Health and Human Services
Social Security Administration

RETIREMENT7/84 $432.70
HOSPITAL 7/84
MEDICAL 7/84

BECAUSE OF A CHANGE IN THE LAW, YOUR REGULAR PAYMENT WILL BE ROUNDED DOWN TO THE DOLLAR EVEN THOUGH YOUR MONTHLY BENEFIT OF RECORD MAY BE IN DOLLARS AND CENTS.

A MONTHLY PREMIUM OF $14.60 IS REQUIRED TO KEEP YOUR MEDICAL INSURANCE PROTECTION. YOU WILL BE BILLED FOR THESE PREMIUMS. YOU WILL RECEIVE YOUR FIRST PREMIUM NOTICE BEFORE */84. AFTER THAT NOTICES WILL BE SENT EVERY 3 MONTHS. THESE NOTICES WILL SHOW THE MONTHS COVERED, TOTAL PREMIUM AMOUNT, AND THE DATE PAYMENT IS DUE.

YOU CANNOT QUALIFY FOR MONTHLY BENEFITS BASED ON ANOTHER PERSON'S SOCIAL SECURITY RECORD WHEN YOU ARE ENTITLED TO AN EQUAL OR LARGER INSURANCE BENEFIT BASED ON YOUR OWN EARNINGS RECORD.

BASED ON THE INFORMATION GIVEN TO US, YOU WERE BORN ON 7/27/19.

IF YOU NEED MEDICARE SERVICES BEFORE YOU RECEIVE YOUR HEALTH INSURANCE CARD, YOU MAY USE THIS NOTICE AS PROOF OF COVERAGE. YOU SHOULD RECEIVE YOUR CARD WITHIN 4 WEEKS.

IF YOU RETIRE FROM YOUR BUSINESS OR CORPORATION BEFORE THE MONTH YOU ATTAIN AGE 70, YOU WILL BE REQUIRED TO PROVIDE EVIDENCE OF YOUR RETIREMENT BEFORE YOUR BENEFITS CAN BE PAID.

YOU ARE NOT ELIGIBLE FOR ANY TYPE OF BENEFIT OTHER THAN STATED ON THIS CERTIFICATE. ENTITLEMENT TO ANOTHER BENEFIT ON THIS OR ANY OTHER RECORD IN THE FUTURE REQUIRES A SEPARATE APPLICATION.

IF YOU BELIVE THIS DETERMINATION IS NOT CORRECT, YOU MAY REQUEST THAT YOUR CASE BE REEXAMINED. IF YOU WANT THIS RECONSIDERATION, YOU MUST REQUEST IT NOT LATER THAN 60 DAYS FROM THE DATE YOU RECEIVE THIS NOTICE. YOU MAY MAKE YOUR REQUEST THROUGH ANY SOCIAL SECURITY OFFICE. IF ADDITIONAL EVIDENCE IS AVIALABLE, YOU SHOULD SUBMIT IT WITH YOUR REQUEST.

This certifies that you (or ther person(s) on whose behalf you applied), became entitled under the Social Security Act to the Social Security benefits shown.

Martha A. McSteen
Acting Commissioner
of Social Security

FIGURE 2-2. **SSA Award Certificate**

From the perspective of the General Counsel's representative, the letter was an adequate representation of the facts about what the law required. From the Systems perspective, it was considered to be as good as the computer could do. But from the clear-writing project staff's perspective, it was a hodgepodge of unclarity, a perspective on which the lawyers and computer specialists fully agreed. All agreed that it desperately needed to be rewritten. This exercise was a milestone in addressing the writing staff's fear about their lowly status in the bureaucracy's pecking order. With their own ears they heard the attorneys and computer people agree with the significance of their work in recasting such notices, a pattern which continued throughout the training sessions.

We next turned our attention to how the offending notice might be recast to make it understandable and to take advantage of the positive fact that SSA was actually awarding money to the reader, and which would give that reader a clear road map of what to do next.

Topic Analysis

We introduced topic analysis at this point. I had found topic analysis of spoken conversation to be extremely helpful in many court cases I had worked on and I suggested that we try it here on the written text before us. Together, we worked out that an examination of the topics revealed the following sequence:

(1) Your payment will be rounded down.
(2) You'll be billed for monthly insurance premiums.
(3) You can't qualify on another person's SS record.
(4) You were born.
(5) Use this notice until you get your health insurance card.
(6) If you retire, provide us with evidence.
(7) You're not eligible for other benefits.
(8) What to do if you disagree with these facts.

Having derived these topics, the participants were then asked to read them sequentially. After a good chuckle, it was pointed out that nowhere in the body of this letter does it say that an award has been made, and yet this is the ostensible reason for the letter in the first place.

Some controversy ensued about the need to tell the readers what their birthdates were. A legal reason could be made for it, but a writing reason could not. It was finally determined that the legal reason could be satisfied by placing this information in a top, right-hand corner, boxed area. It was also decided that one number currently appearing in that box, the amount of the monthly check, was too important to be relegated to that area and should be incorporated in the text itself.

But why, the participants asked, should the rounding down of the amount of the check be placed first in the text? No adequate answer was given. Perhaps none was possible.

What became clear from the discussion of this notice was that a topic analysis strategy was a useful first step in deciding how to revise this notice. All participants agreed that the purpose of the letter should be noted first and that rounding down in no way met that purpose. This led us to develop together a set of topic analysis strategies, as follows:

(1) Determine the purpose of the notice and front this topic.
(2) Determine the main idea of each paragraph.
(3) Write down these main ideas, as in the topic analysis above.
(4) Read the resulting list of topic, or main, ideas.
(5) Determine whether the sequence of these topics is appropriate. If not, resequence them until it is.
(6) Determine whether this sequence captures the reader's perspective. If not, revise until it does.

The reader's perspective was determined from the results of the participants' fieldwork or homework assignments. When they found their SSA recipients to interview with the notice, they asked them, among other things, what they wanted to hear from SSA. They found, to a person, that recipients wanted to know the following three things: (1) Am I going to get any money? (2) How much? (3) When? There were no other questions from the recipient perspective. SSA may want or need to tell them other things, but these are the things the recipients wanted to hear. This was their perspective.

Topic analysis, then, became an important first step in all notices analyzed by the participants in the training program. By analyzing the topics in existing notices that were being revised, it became clear to the participants that there are several types of topic marking. Staton and I did not need to lecture about this point. The data made it obvious to the participants, one of the beauties of our hands-on approach.

The approach that I had used in my revision of the congressionally mandated Medicare benefits notice (see Chapter 1) was the question-answer framework. In this approach, the question is asked in the voice of the recipient, as in "How can I get more Social Security funds?" and answered in the voice of SSA. The question-answer (Q-A) approach can be very useful because it obviously captures the participant's perspective, but it would tend to become tedious if all correspondence from SSA were in that format. For this reason, Staton and I proposed a set of topic-marking alternatives, as follows:

(1) Performatives.

Examples: "This notice is to inform you that . . . "
"You will be receiving $435 a month . . . "
"Your benefits will stop on October 3 . . . "
"Your benefits will increase from $345 to $450 . . . "

(2) Headings.

Examples: Your Social Security Benefits
Amount of Payment
Your Eligibility for Other Benefits

The headings format calls attention to the topic as the heading and uses the voice of SSA instead of the recipient.

(3) Question-Answer. As noted earlier, this approach speaks in the voice of the recipient, not that of SSA.

Examples: How much money will I get?
How did you figure my payment?
How can I find out more?

(4) Embedded in text (but not performatively). Whereas the performative format explicitly states what the topic is, the embedded format is more indirect. This format is common in most writing.

Examples: "Your attorney must send us a copy of the bill and we must approve it."
"In April 1985, we will look at your case again to see if your disability has gotten better."

(5) Implied in text. These topics are neither performative nor embedded topics, often appearing in the letterhead or in a boxed area of the notice.

Examples: Social Security Award Certificate (on letterhead).
Monthly Benefit Amount (in box at top). Often simply stated as an amount, such as $432.27.

By our calling attention to these five ways of indicating the topic, the participants became aware of alternative strategies of topic marking in order to then select the one most appropriate for the type of notice under consideration for revision. Sometimes simply identifying one's options makes the process clearer.

As a revision strategy, then, topic analysis has a great deal to offer. By providing a holistic macropicture of the entire letter, rather than a word or individual sentence picture, topic analysis causes the revisor to find and front the main idea of the letter, to sequence the topics in a logical way and from the reader's perspective, and to mark the topics in the most appropriate manner.

The Decision Tree

One of the important outcomes of the fieldwork assignment was that the participants asked the SSA recipients what they thought they were to do as a result of having received the notice. Not surprisingly, there was large scale indecision. However, there was complete agreement among the clear-writing participants that SSA's notices should give clear guidance to recipients about their alternative courses of action. The problem then was articulated as, "How do we provide a clear road map of the appropriate action a recipient can take?" This led to our developing together a decision tree, a kind of outline map of the alternatives available and the choices that a recipient might make. The following is an example. When revising an award notice, for example, the following steps are taken:

(1) Chart all topics.
(2) Arrange topics as a flow chart, with three column categories: SSA propositions, decision points, and reader actions.
(3) Arrange the chart as the example in Figure 2-3 indicates:

If a notice can be outlined with the clarity above, there is a good chance that the road map will be clear to the reader. If not, the writer should revise until the map is clear. Oddly enough, our training program sometimes revealed that even the writer was unclear about the map.

Speech Acts

Another linguistic contribution to the training sessions consisted of our introducing some rudimentary aspects of speech acts. We pointed out that speech act analysis can be very useful in considering how to revise a notice since, of all the available linguistic units of analysis, such as phonology, morphology, syntax, and discourse, speech acts are the closest to the kind of intentionality that seemed to undergird this problem. The writers

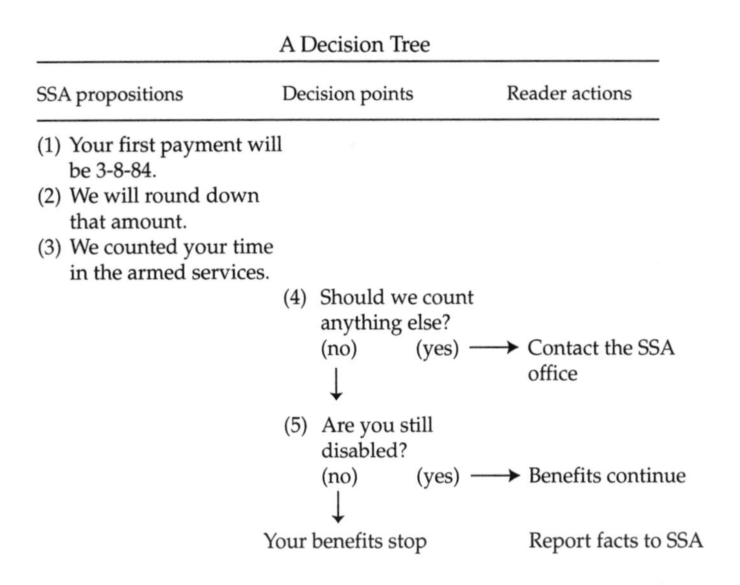

FIGURE 2-3. Decision Tree

needed to figure out the intention of the documents they were trying to revise and to predict the reactions of the unseen recipients.

As usual, we began with actual notices brought in by the participants. We pointed out that people use language to get things done, such as promising, denying, giving directives, complaining, offering, reporting facts, apologizing, warning, threatening, advising, and requesting. We noted that a notice might contain the speech act of warning, for example, when the writer merely wanted to be giving advice. It might also give a directive when the writer intended to offer an option. We debated the appropriateness of various speech acts in the context of SSA notices and concluded that SSA should probably not threaten. The participants categorized the speech acts as positive versus negative types of messages, with threatening, complaining, warning, denying, and even giving directives as potentially, if not actually, negative in their thrust. It is one thing to know that bureaucratic writing should be as positive as possible, in that it represents possible political ramifications, but it is quite another thing to learn to be able to spot what makes for negativity and, perhaps more important, what could replace it. Even when the notice requires a negative speech act, such as denying a claim, there are ways to soften such denial. Especially in the public sector, it is important that appropriate tone be achieved. Most of the participants could spot a problematic tone, but they had more difficulty in determining exactly what was out of joint about it. Speech act analysis provided one tool for them.

We also leapt into the difficult waters of indirect speech acts and sincerity conditions, practicing giving each other both types of language in the sessions, such as "I guess I goofed," offered as a dubiously sincere apology, and "Can you reach that window," given as an indirect request. The participants enjoyed this greatly and one facetiously commented that he now understood how administrators at SSA got where they are.

Indirectness is often favored in social interactions, but in administrative writing, being direct in a polite way helps keep the readers from misreading. They should not be required to infer what SSA wishes or suggests in the way of actions.

Consider the following revision of an earlier SSA notice. One participant in our group adopted the Q-A format, largely because this is a one-time letter (to be sent out only once) that would not lose its impact because of overfamiliarity with the format. The revisor numbered, on the left, the speech acts that he found in this notice.

(1) You may be able to get more money because of a recent court decision about Supplemental Security Income (SSI).
(2) These questions and answers will help you decide if the court decision applies to you.
(3) **What did the court say?**
(4) The court said that we have to change the way we figure how much SSI we pay to some people.
(5) The change applies only to married couples living together in Massachusetts at some time since January 1977.
(6) **Does the court decision mean that any couple can get more SSI?**
(7) No.
(8) The only couples who may get more money are those where only one person got SSI and the other person had income.
(9) **What if both of us are getting SSI?**
(10) Then the court decision won't change what you get from SSI.
(11) **Will the court decision raise my SSI if I'm not married now?**
(12) If you were married at any time since January 1977, the court decision may apply to you.
(13) **Could the court decision change?**
(14) Another court may be looking at this decision.
(15) If there is a new court decision, the way we have to figure your payments may change again.
(16) **I have been getting SSI for some time. Does the court's decision mean I can get back benefits?**
(17) Yes. We can refigure your benefits as far back as January 1977. If we owe you money because of this, we will pay you.
(20) **If I think I can get more SSI money, what do I do?**

(21) Call or visit your Social Security office right away.
(22) Look in the telephone book for the office closest to you.
(23) If you visit our office, be sure to bring this paper with you.
(24) It will help us answer your questions.

A revision-oriented speech act analysis of this letter first asks the analyst to mark all speech acts. The resulting sequence of speech acts, as numbered above by the participant, is as follows:

(1) Offer
(2) Promise
(3) Question
(4) Report fact
(5) Report fact
(6) Question
(7) Report fact
(8) Report fact
(9) Question
(10) Report fact
(11) Question
(12) Report fact
(13) Question
(14) Report fact
(15) Give advice
(16) Question
(17) Report fact
(18) Offer
(19) Promise
(20) Question
(21) Offer
(22) Give advice
(23) Give advice
(24) Report fact

The revisor proudly noted that he had included no negative speech acts, and that he had advised rather than warned or threatened. He also pointed out that he had provided complex information in the best way he could think of. The point here, however, is not so much the success or failure of this attempt at revising, as much as it is to point out how participants were encouraged to think of the speech acts in their writing as a way to guide their ultimate products. In the training sessions, we had the participants write the speech acts on the text itself but, for the sake of printing clarity here, we used the number referencing system above.

Speech act analysis of more problematic SSA notices led to a discussion of politeness, indirectness, and eventually to the kinds of speech acts that are most appropriate for a government bureaucracy to use. The participants took the notion of positive and negative speech acts to construct the categories for their own future use as shown in Figure 2-4.

They understood these categories to be suggestive, not absolute. They called to our attention that in notices that deny the recipients' claims to eligibililty, negativity was absolutely necessary. This is, of course, quite true. This fact led us to understand, however, that what we mean by avoiding negatives is actually that we should avoid unnecessary negatives. Some are actually necessary, as the following indicate:

(1) If you are not a class member, the new law does **not** apply to you.
(2) Attorney fees will **not** be held back from any benefits you receive while we are reviewing your case.

Potentially negative	Neutral	Positive, polite
Warning	Reporting facts	Offering
Complaining	RequestinG information	Promising
Giving directives		Thanking
Threatening		Congratulating
		Inviting
		Sympathizing
		Advising
		Greeting
		Questions from the reader's perspective
		Closing

FIGURE 2-4. **Positive, Neutral, Negative Speech Acts**

(3) You will **not** be asked to pay back any Medicare benefits you get while we review your case.

Number one is in reference to a class action suit in which it was necessary to determine whether or not the reader was a member of that class. Several preceding sentences had identified what it meant to be a class member and now, to be completely clear, the notice contrasts such membership in a possibly negative way. Numbers two and three are statements which, although using negatives, actually have a positive outcome since the result to the readers is positive and the negative works to their advantage.

On the other hand, many statements in the original SSA notices were unnecessarily negative, as shown in Figure 2-4.

Our SSA trainees agreed that their agency should be as positive and, of course, as polite, as possible. Much of the task of the SSA notice-writer is to provide and request information, a neutral speech act by their definition, neither positive nor negative. They also agreed that whenever it is possible to couch information positively (Figure 2-5), this is preferred to stating it negatively. It also became quite clear that when the reader was given a type of action to take, more powerful speech acts, such as directives or even advice and warnings, might well be the appropriate stance to take, especially if these were framed with politeness.

In terms of a procedure for notice-writers to follow as they revise extant letters, we devised the following suggestions:

(a) For a given notice, mark all the speech acts on the text (in the margins or over the sentences).

Negative original	Positive revision
Your case **will not** be reviewed unless you ask us to	We will review your case if you ask us to.
We **can't pay** you for any month before the court returned the class action suit.	We can pay you only for months after the class action suit began.

FIGURE 2-5. **Comparison of Negative and Positive Speech Acts**

(b) Think about the intention of the notice. Do the speech acts marked best reflect SSA's intentions? If not, modify the speech acts (make indirect ones direct, if appropriate, and replace negative speech acts with neutral or positive ones where possible).
(c) Think about the speech acts that the reader needs in order to respond effectively to the notice. If necessary, modify the speech acts accordingly.

More specific to the special problems created by past SSA notices, the following checklist was developed:

(1) Does the notice warn when it should advise?
(2) Does the notice offer, invite, or promise appropriately?
(3) Does the notice threaten or warn unnecessarily?
(4) Does the notice give directives when the intent of SSA is to offer alternatives or options?
(5) Are the speech acts unnecessarily negative?

Discourse Analysis

In developing this checklist, we were guided by Grice's maxims of communicative cooperation (Grice 1975). These maxims were presented to the participants and were applied to their written products. Grice observed that communicative exchanges do not normally consist of a succession of disconnected remarks and would not be rational if they did. Our talk is characteristically a cooperative effort and each participant in conversation recognizes, to some extent, a common purpose or set of purposes, or at least a mutually accepted direction. This may be fixed from the start or it may evolve during the exchanges. But at each stage some possible conversational moves would be excluded as conversationally unsuitable. We translated Grice's maxims into the bureaucratic context as follows: Make your communicative contribution such as is required by the accepted purpose or direction of the communication in which you are engaged, with the following "rules" that allow us to make sense out of what we are communicating: (1) Informativeness, no more and no less; (2) Relevance; (3) Sincerity, in this case accuracy (rather than Grice's truthfulness); and (4) Clarity, avoiding obscurity and ambiguity while maintaining orderliness.

By no means did we expect the trainees to become experts in discourse analysis, speech acts, Grice's maxims, or any other contribution of linguistics to their work. But we found that even the rough ideas that we were able to present gave them a new and more explanatory way of thinking about their task of creating clear writing.

Once we had introduced discourse analysis and speech acts as a way of thinking about their tasks, we turned our attention to cohesion, something that was clearly lacking in many, if not most, of the notices that the participants brought to class. Several of the writers had noted, in their words, that their notice did not "hang together." As we explored what they meant by this, we suggested "cohesion" as the missing ingredient. They liked this word, making it easy for us to introduce Halliday and Hassan's (1976) notion of cohesive ties. We briefly discussed five types of cohesive ties: reference, substitution, ellipsis, conjunction, and lexical. We took actual notices that the participants were working with and together we marked all cohesive ties and drew arrows from them to the words to which they were semantically connected. This visual approach proved to be quite effective, for soon the participants also began to see where better cohesive ties could have been used in the original documents.

At this point, it should be noted that having marked up their notices for discourse, speech acts, negative verbs, and now cohesive ties, the documents were becoming filled with edits and were nearly unreadable. To remedy this, we suggested that they bring in several copies of their notices and engage in the common practice linguists follow of making several passes through the same text, once for one feature and then for another. As simple and obvious such a procedure is to linguists, who are used to it, it is often news to people in other fields.

An example of difficulty with one type of cohesive tie, lexical cohesion, can be seen in the last paragraph of the complete notice cited at the beginning of this chapter:

> If you believe this determination is not correct, you may request a **reexamination**. If you want this **reconsideration**, you must **request** it not later than 60 days from the date you receive this notice. You may make your request through any Social Security Office. If additional evidence is available, you should submit it with your request.

As is evident, three different terms are used to refer to a process that the reader may request: **reexamination**, **reconsideration**, and, arguably perhaps, **request**. However elegant it may be to use synonyms, such synonyms can work against clarity in good administrative writing. This is true largely because the reader can never be sure exactly what constitutes a term of art in the writing of the sender. It is not clear whether these three terms refer to the same thing. If the recipient were to write to SSA in response to this notice, which term should be used? Such issues can be unsuspecting traps, as was illustrated in my own recent experience with an insurance company. One question asked whether or not I was "sponsoring" my college-aged son. My first reaction was to say "yes." What father would not sponsor his son? But my awareness of terms of art in general caused me to hesitate and to ask what was meant by "sponsor." It turns out that a "yes" answer would have doubled my monthly premium, since "sponsoring," to the insurance industry, means that my son would be added to my policy as a nongroup participant, rather than as a group participant.

By examining an SSA notice for cohesive ties such as "reexamination" and "reconsideration," the trainees were able to see a difficulty from the reader's perspective and they eventually agreed on a single term to be used consistently to refer to the object of this request.

The topic of cohesion also provided the opportunity to consider linguistic notions of coreference and presupposition: one element in the text presupposes the other and cannot be decoded without recourse to it. We took Grice's work on presupposition (1975) and developed three checklist questions that the clear-writing project could use when they were revising notices:

(1) Is the presupposed assertion actually clear and true for this situation?
(2) Is what is presupposed likely to be known and understood by most readers?
(3) Would it help the clarity and comprehensibility of the notice if the presupposed assertions were made explicit?

Finally, the concept of cohesive ties led to a revision strategy procedure which the participants could use as they worked on their notices:

(1) Mark the cohesive ties in the notice.
(2) Draw arrows to the defined referent of each cohesive tie, even if it is in a previous paragraph.
(3) Ask yourself what possible misreadings or misunderstandings might result from any existing or missing cohesive ties.

(4) Add or modify existing cohesive ties that avoid such misreading or misunderstanding.
(5) Examine the notice for external (across-paragraph) cohesion as well as for internal (within-paragraph) cohesion.

Word Comprehension

The training program deliberately focused on the discourse and syntactic strategies of clear writing before examining the more conventional ideas about word comprehension. It proved somewhat difficult to defer word analysis since some of the participants, especially those with some background in English or education, kept wanting to discuss things with which they were more familiar, the surface level, visible word choice decisions. We observed that there is nothing wrong with a concern for word level comprehension and that this was also important. In our view, however, it is better to deal with the larger elements of discourse, speech acts, and syntax before one addresses the more micro word level. Our view is that there is no point in being worried about word comprehension if the discourse or sentence units lack comprehensibility. We wanted to work on the big things first, then move to the smaller ones.

Our focus on word comprehension relied heavily on work that had gone on before us, particularly on that of the Document Design (Reddish 1981), but not excluding some of the more conventional knowledge in the field of composition. For example, we emphasized the need to try to stick to the simple present, past, and future tenses (we pretended that there actually is a future tense in English, for the sake of the participants). We stressed the need to avoid switching tenses inappropriately, as the following older version of an SSA notice managed to do:

> Before the law changed, it had been the right of all recipients to . . ., or you may have been informed previously that . . . , or by next year, you will have been paid.

We also stressed the need to include causal relators and to not rely on the reader's ability to infer a connection which is not made explicit, as the following contrast shows:

Old version:	*Revision:*
There is a new law. We are reducing your amount.	We are reducing your amount **because** of a new law.

The old two-sentence version produced a high score on the readability formula in use at that time (SSA has subsequently reduced its reliance on any readability formula), but it certainly lacked the explicit causal connector which, though it produced a longer sentence and a lower readability formula score, also created a less comprehensible text.

Many other word comprehension issues were addressed, all based on the text of existing SSA notices, including the following:

(1) "Which-that" relators should be included, e.g. "We feel the best thing to do is . . . " vs. "We feel that the best thing to do is . . . "
(2) Preposition relator should be included, e.g. "past year's income" vs. "income for the past year."
(3) The use of positive rather than negative constructions, e.g. "Please remember" vs. "Don't forget."
(4) The use of active rather than passive constructions.
(5) Limiting the use of "shall" and "must" (too directive).
(6) The use of animate nouns rather than abstract ones, e.g. "money" vs. "resources."
(7) Avoid terms of art which may not be understood as terms of art by the reader.
(8) The use of verbs rather than compound nouns.
(9) The use of animate nouns rather than inanimate ones, e.g. "your husband" vs. "a relative."

Authority Based on Linguistic Justification

All such choices, of course, are generalizations and are dependent on contextual constraints. It may be necessary, for example, to use the passive voice in some circumstances. The danger of such lists resides in the false assumption that they are fixed rules rather than general guidelines.

Earlier we noted that the final notice sent out by SSA was the product of many influences. First of all, notices are a direct result of congressional laws, and so the agency must be careful to carry out the law fully and accurately. Attorneys, whose language often seems to differ markedly from that of other people, have a deep concern for the actual wording of all correspondence coming from SSA. Their authority is based on the law, or their interpretation of it. Their task is to keep it within its bounds. Policy specialists have the authority of SSA procedures and practices based on interpretations of that law, often in the form of regulations. Their concern is that SSA correspondence not be inconsistent with such policies. Computer systems specialists also have an authority based on the existence and capability of the computer's hardware and software. For instance, at the onset of our training, SSA's computers were limited to using only capital letters despite the fact that document design psychologists and linguists have long held that readers have great difficulty with documents printed in all capitals.

When SSA decided to make clear writing one of its priorities, these authority bases clearly had precedence over whatever authority an individual writer might claim. One major goal of the training program, then, was to establish a competing authority, a credibility, a muscle for the writers to give them equal, or at least some, footing in this important decision-making process. In order to do this, the writers needed to be able to offer theory and knowledge-based grounds for their choices. If clear writing meant anything, they had to be able to justify their procedures not only to their own group, but also to the others. This was, of course, the major reason why we insisted that the training participants come from all four areas of SSA.

The activities of the training program partially described here led to the formulation of this ability to justify the revisions they made. The last training sessions, in fact, required the participants to justify to their superiors why they had made these revisions. As an aid to this procedure, we developed a Notice Review Guide which could be used as a checklist for such a justification (see Figure 2-5). It does not include all the points covered in the training program or all the points possible to imagine. To do so would be unwieldy, of course. The points included, however, were the ones which came up repeatedly in the participants' analyses of the documents they were working on, and they were ones considered by the participants to be most crucial.

Figure 2-6 is the Notice Review Guide developed.

Conclusion

A number of approaches to the language policy issues at SSA might have been attempted. SSA could have tried to farm out its writing problems to consultants outside the agency. It could have followed the insurance industry by simply applying readability formulas to its written communications, achieving only word comprehension, if that. It could have denied that there was a problem at all. It could have engaged in petty bickering among subcomponents of the agency—General Counsel, Systems, Policy, and the writing staff. We actually expected such bickering when we began our training, but we never actually experienced any.

Instead, SSA admitted its weakness, co-opted the linguist who had been

Notice Review Guide

Categories possible	No changes made	Changes made	Further changes
Topics:			
Topics fronted:			
Topics marked:			
Headings:			
Question-Answer:			
Embedded in 1st sentence:			
Topics sequenced appropriately:			
Explicitness:			
Ambiguities, inference, presupposition made explicit:			
Reader decision points clarified:			
Reader actions specified:			
Speech/Acts			
Speech acts made appropriate to message intention:			
Speech acts made positive:			
Speech acts made explicit:			
Cohesion:			
Cohesive ties added appropriately:			
Pronoun referencing improved:			
Relationship markers added or changed:			
Lexical repetition added:			
Comprehension:			
Concrete words replace abstract words:			
Active voice replaces passive voice:			
Relative pronouns included:			

FIGURE 2-6. **Notice Review Guide**

working against them in a lawsuit, asked for help, created a well-protected administrative entity that nurtured the project, took the advice of the trainers, and implemented a new language policy that had at least the strong potential for continuation. During the two or three years after our training ended, we noticed a distinct improvement in the quality of the notices sent out by SSA. Now, well over a decade later, many of the people we trained have moved on to other positions within and outside the agency and it is difficult to determine any long-range effects. It is hoped that the computer has stored most of the revisions that grew out of our work and that they continue to be sent out. But even if our impact was short-lived, it shows that language policy in a bureaucracy can, indeed, be changed.

Chapter 3

A Bureaucracy's Struggle with Saying "No": A Medicare Case Study

Giving someone bad news has long been regarded as one of the most difficult of human language tasks. Doctors stumble, use the passive voice, employ indirectness, and generally try to avoid the problem of telling patients that they have a terminal illness. Teachers find it hard sometimes to give bad grades to their students, leading, perhaps, to the current complaints about grade inflation. Marriage partners who have given up on their marriage often find it excruciatingly hard to tell their mates that everything is over. The speech act of denying is never an easy one to accomplish, especially for a government bureaucracy that was established to provide benefits to the public it serves. Yet, just as doctors have to be truthful about their patients' true condition, it is often necessary for bureaucracies to say "no" to beneficiaries. How they do this can prove problematic, as is portrayed in the following case.

Being Denied a Claim for Medicare

Shortly after our work began training the Clear Writing Staff at (SSA), the National Senior Citizens Law Center came back with another problem for me, this time with a document called Notice of Medicare Claim Determination. A staff attorney for the Gray Panthers, Sally Hart Wilson, observed that the notice did not indicate which of a number of possible reasons for disallowance were applied when the recipient was denied a claim. Perhaps more significantly, the language used in the notice seemed to her to require a higher reading level ability than the average Medicare beneficiary might possess. This notice is reproduced in its entirety in Figure 3-1 (but note that this notice appears on two sides of the same paper, the second side starting with the numbered paragraphs).

Everything that was said about the general unfriendly, impersonal, and incomprehensible nature of the Social Security notices discussed earlier is multiplied by this notice. The document is designed for the needs and purposes of the agency, not the recipient. In addition to attorney Wilson's observations about its lack of reason for denial and general unreadability, I reported the following.

Title

The content of the notice is, in essence, a disapproval of claim, yet its title gives no hint of this denial. It is very tempting for doctors to disguise bad news that their dying patients have to learn. Children often paint a bright picture about what they are doing well in school before showing their parents a disappointing report card. But eventually the truth comes out. In the case of this Medicare denial of the beneficiary's claim, there appears to be such an effort to disguise the bad news. Logic would tell us that titles ought to reflect the content of a document which, in this case, denies the beneficiary's claim. One need look no further than the efforts of commercial manufacturers to see a precedent. Labels on hazardous products are required by law to describe the dangers therein but they do so reluctantly at best, worrying that if consumers should happen to read this warning they might be dissuaded from buying the product. So manufacturers do their best to disguise their words, all the time keeping, or attempting to keep, within the U.S. Food and Drug Administration (FDA) guidelines. All we can tell from the title of the notice discussed here is that a "determination" will follow somewhere in the text. While it is true that denial is one type of determination, there is no particular reason to keep the readers in suspense until they finally figure this one out. It is clearly a denial form. I suggested changing the title to "Notice of Claim Disapproval" or "Notice of Non-Allowance of Your Claim."

Notice of Medicare Claim Determination
Intermediary Number, Name and Address

Date ______
Your Health Insurance
Claim No. ______

Services Provided By: (Name and Address)

Provider Number

Type of Service Provided PERIOD O Hospital O Skilled Nursing Facility O Home Health O Other ______ Agency	Date of Admission or First Visit:	NOTICE COVERS PERIOD	
		FROM	THROUGH
	Insurance O Hospital O Medical		

This concerns the services you received from the facility shown above. Medicare cannot pay for the above services for the following reasons:

Extended care benefits are paid under Medicare for individuals who need, on a daily basis, skilled nursing care or skilled rehabilitation services which as a practical matter can only be provided in a skilled nursing facility on an inpatient basis. Patients must require such extended care services for the continued treatment of a condition for which they received medically necessary inpatient hospital care or for a condition which arose while they were in a skilled nursing facility receiving care for the same condition for which they received inpatient hospital services. Skilled care is the type of care which must be furnished by or under the supervision of skilled personnel to assure the safety of the patient and to achieve the medically desired result.

When individuals do not require such skilled services on a daily basis, or when as a practical matter the provision of such services does not require that the individuals be admitted as inpatients to a skilled nursing facility, their care in a skilled nursing facility is not covered under the Medicare law. Since we have determined that the care you received was not the type described, no Medicare hospital insurance benefits can be allowed for your skilled nursing facility stay.

HOWEVER, your responsibility for payment of services received has been relieved because of a special provision in the Social Security Act. See paragraph ____1 ____2 on the reverse of this notice for more information on the waiver of liability provisions which pertains to this claim.

Important: See other side for an explanation of your appeal rights and other information.

1. Despite an adverse determination concerning noncovered services, program payment is being made under the waiver of liability provisions. This provision of the law permits payment when it has been determined that neither you nor the provider knew or had reason to know that the services received were not covered under Medicare. Since this is the finding in your case, for those dates where your responsibility for payment of services received has been relieved, you are liable only for the deductible, coinsurance, and any charges for services or items normally not covered by Medicare. The receipt of this notice is considered evidence that you are aware the the services you received were not covered. Therefore, you will not be protected from liability for such services in the future if it is determined they involve treatment for the same condition or a similar level of care.

   Even though payment is being made, if you disagree with the coverage determination, you may request reconsideration as explained in this notice.

FIGURE 3-1. Notice of Medicare Claim Determination

2. Despite an adverse determination concerning noncovered services, a provision of the law relieves a beneficiary from liability for payment for such noncovered services when it is determined that the beneficiary neither knew nor had reason to know that services received were not covered under Medicare. Thus, for those dates where your responsibility for payment of services received has been relieved you are liable only for the deductible, coinsurance, and any charges for services or items normally not covered by Medicare. Also, the number of days and/or visits used during the waived period will be charged against your Medicare utilization record. If you have already paid the provider for the services, please contact this office or your local Social Security office within 6 months of the date of this notice and furnish the following documents: a copy of this notice, the bill received for services, receipts or other evidence of payments to the provider.

   The receipt of this notice is considered evidence that you are aware that the services you received were not covered. Therefore, you will not be protected from liability for such services in the future if it is determined they involve treatment for the same condition or a similar level of care. Even though you are not liable for the billed services described above, if you disagree with the coverage determination, you may request a reconsideration as explained in this notice.

   If you have any questions about this notice, you should first get a detailed explanation from you Social Security office. If you still believe the determination is not correct, you may make a request for reconsideration for Hospital insurance (or a review for Medical insurance). For Hospital insurance, you must file your request within 60 days from the date of receipt of this notice. For Medical insurance, you must file your request for a review 6 months from the date of this notice. You may make your request through your Social Security office.

   Rev. 694 3-245.8

FIGURE 3-1. (continued)

Sentence Structure

The first sentence begins with "This," naked and undefined by any preceding defined reference. It may seem obvious that it means "this notice" but it never hurts to be clear about it and, of course, without such clarification there is no explicit defined referent; only an inferable one. The dangers of causing readers to have to infer meaning are legion, as any civil attorney knows.

In terms of readability, the conventional way to approach attorney Wilson's observation that it might tax the reading level ability to Medicare recipients is to apply one or more of the available readability formulas. Most such formulas are based on the assumption that short words and sentences are more readable than long ones. One could count the number of sentences, then divide this into the total number of words. In this case one would find that the average sentence length of this notice is almost thirty words, quite long indeed. Although it is true that long sentences may prove difficult to process, it is not length alone that is the problem. Sentence length, however, is only the surface of the issue, and does not explain the reasons for the complexity that might make sentences long in the first place. The "short is better than long" theory, for example, would mark the word, "sphinx," as easier to read than "merry-go-round," a preposterous notion at best. It is equally possible to dream up short but hard to understand sentences and long but highly comprehensible ones. The major problem is not so much the length of sentences as their complexity.

Paragraph two of this notice begins with a forty-word sentence containing nine layers of embedded clauses and prepositional phrases as idea separators. One way to display this is as follows:

"Extended care benefits are paid
  under Medicare
    for individuals
      -who need
        on a daily basis
      -skilled nursing care or skilled rehabilitation services
        -which
          as a practical matter
        -can only be provided
          in a skilled nursing facility
            on an inpatient basis."

Note that six of the forty words in this sentence are prepositions. This yields an average of 6.6 prepositions, far denser than clear writing dictates. By comparison, James J. Kilpatrick, a syndicated columnist regarded as a clear writer, averages one preposition every 14.9 words.

The second sentence in this paragraph contains forty-nine words with seven layers of embedding. It used seven prepositions, one of every seven words. The third sentence has eight layers of embedding in thirty-three words, with a ratio of one preposition every 6.7 words.

Note that ten of the twenty-five sentences in this notice begin with dependent clauses: "when," "since," "despite," "even though," and the favorite, "if." Clear administrative writing fronts the main idea, not the subordinate one. The paragraph marked "1." begins with a subordinate clause while the important point, from the reader's perspective, is at the end of the second sentence of that section ("you didn't know that you were not covered"). These two sentences say, essentially, that the law permits us to pay you when you were unaware that you were not covered. What the readers are most interested in is, first, that they will be paid and, only secondly if at all, that the reason for this is that the law permits it. The writing of this notice consistently takes the sender's perspective rather than the receiver's, a violation of good administrative prose style.

The paragraph marked "2." omits pronouns that might clarify the attribution and lead to comprehensibility. For example, "Despite an adverse determination concerning noncovered services" is an unclear, shorthand, pronoun-deficient way of saying, "Even though we reject your claim for your non-covered services." This and other administrative notices tend to avoid attribution of actions by fogging them with nominals or the passive voice rather than accepting responsibility more openly with personal pronouns.

Conveyed Meaning

Of course, a writer can never be sure that the meaning intended will be understood in the same way. But there are ways to guard against misunderstandings of this sort. It is problematic to assume that merely saying something accomplishes a goal. In the second paragraph of "2.," for example, this notice says, "The receipt of this notice is considered evidence that you are aware that the services you received were not covered." Can the receipt of a notice be evidence of awareness? Does the U.S. Department of Health and Human Services mean that recipients actually know what is intended simply because it is sent and received? Is this some way of avoiding saying what is really intended here, such as, "From the time you get this notice, **we** consider **our** responsibility to inform **you** now completed"? It appears that the agency once again shifts the focus away from its own action of explaining to the readers their responsibility to understand this. It is possible that legal considerations compel the agency to put their readers on notice of the importance of this document and the finality of this decision. But it boggles the mind to believe that the writers can, through writing, construct "evidence" of awareness.

Vocabulary choice is perhaps the most obvious thing that can cause reader confusion. It is hoped that recipients of government notices will not have to use a dictionary (if they even have one) to translate the words found in the notices. Nor can they be expected to understand the terms of art common to the sender of the message, such as "waiver," "Medicare utilization record," "relieved," "adverse determination," "a reconsideration," and "a review." It is poor judgment in administrative writing to use terms of art, or even expressions that may be construed as terms of art, in notices of this sort. The English language has a large stock of clear words available.

Conclusion

My review of the problems with this notice was reported to HHS and, after considerable negotiation, most of the suggestions were incorporated into a revised notice. Once again, it is possible to discover that even one of the most specialized, hierarchical proliferated, and red tape-bound bureaucracies, such as HHS, could be moved to a clearer, consumer-oriented position. It is unfortunate that it takes a lawsuit, or at least a threat of one, to bring such things about. But bureaucracies are difficult to change, and without watchdog organizations like the National Senior Citizens Law Center, one might not expect much change at all. On the other hand, I have also found that the encrusted layerings of some bureaucracies do not want to be as hard-hearted as they may, on occasion, seem. Once one gets to the actual people inside the bureaucracies, one finds many warm and well-intentioned human beings who will do better if they can only figure out how. Linguistic analysis aides in such matters, primarily by giving not only suggestions about how to be clear and accurate, but also about how to justify such revisions with the authority of language practice. Such knowledge is, in a very real way, power and authority. Without it, writers can be, and often are, placed in a non-authoritative, one-down position by the supposedly unimpeachable authority of other bureaucrats in the agencies.

Chapter 4

When Bureaucracies Clash: A Case Study of Physicians' Disability Report Forms

Sometimes the language issues of the bureaucracy stem from the way bureaucrats communicate with the outside world. But there are also times when bureaucracies such as the Social Security Administration (SSA) have trouble getting internal and external bureaucracies to communicate effectively with them. Such a situation arose in Tennessee on April 8, 1987, when SSA ordered the Tennessee Disability Determination Section (TDDS), which performs disability evaluations for SSA, to obtain more information from treating physicians. Here we find a clash between two different users of bureaucratic language, the government and the medical profession.

The Clash of Bureaucracies

The bureaucratic language of physicians, including the hierarchy of authority, specialization of functions, adherence to fixed rules, and red tape officialdom, has been well documented (Nader and Maretzki 1973; Barber 1980; Fisher and Todd 1983; Mishler 1984; West 1984; Fisher 1986; Todd 1989). Bureaucratic language commonly becomes a problem for people outside that bureaucracy. In this case we find the specialized language of medicine, along with its authoritarian asymmetry, butting heads with the specialized language of government, along with its own version of authoritarian asymmetry. Neither seems to be particularly concerned with the perspective of the other, at least not from any past indication, and both are positioned to be in charge. The cloying question, "Why should we do it any differently from before?" could easily be asked by both sides in this case. TDDS, being a dutiful bureaucracy, had no choice but to follow SSA's order. Physicians, not feeling the same sense of duty, since the order did not come from their own bureaucracy, might not have wished to be so compliant.

TDDS's Proposed Medical Assessment Report Form

Although the order from SSA was reasonably detailed as to what was to be asked, there was nothing in that order about the format to be used, as follows:

Duty to Obtain Medical Assessments

> The Tennessee Disability Determinations Section (TDDS) shall obtain the medical assessments required by 20 C.F.R. SS 404.1513 and 416.913 from each treating and consulting physician from whom evidence is acquired. These assessments shall be complete enough to allow a determination of residual functional capacity and, at a minimum, shall request how many hours in an eight-hour day a claimant can walk, stand, and sit and how much weight can be lifted for one-third and two-thirds of a work day. . . . This information is to be complete enough to allow TDDS to make a determination of the claimant's residual functional capacity (RFC).

In response to this order, Tennessee Disability Determinations Section developed its own report form (here referred to as Form A) and put it into use. Legal Services of Middle Tennessee (Legal Services), a watchdog organization, objected to this form and attempted to produce an improved version. Their effort, in fact, produced two alternative forms (here referred to as Forms B and C). Unable to decide which of these two to suggest to TDDS, one of the attorneys at Legal Services of Middle Tennessee, Russ Overby, contacted me for help. Figure 4-1 shows the form first put in place by TDDS, exactly reproduced in every respect except for letterhead, address of recipient, date, and time.

The form that TDDS had been using, Form A, is vintage SSA document

TDDS, Form A

MEDICAL ASSESSMENT

TO: RE: A/M:

In your report or in this space, indicate whether your patient's impairment(s) affects the ability to do work-related activities. If so, describe your patient's remaining ability to do work-related activities such as sitting, standing, moving about, lifting, carrying, handling objects, hearing, speaking, and traveling. In mental impairment cases, please describe the ability to reason or make occupational, personal, or social adjustments.

Describe your patient's abilities in terms of the maximum total time that he/she can spend doing that activity during an 8-hour work day rather than as a continual activity. Activities involving strength and endurance should be quantified in terms of weight, time, and distance based on your medical judgment of what your patient can do. At a minimum, specific information is needed about how many hours the individual can walk, stand, and sit in an 8-hour day. Also, we need to know, based on the individual's impairment(s) how much weight can be lifted for one-third and two-thirds of a work day. If the impairment(s) does not cause any limitations in strength, or lifting, please so state. Your report should contain the medical basis for the abilities or limitations you desribe.

____

____

____

____

____

____

____

____

____

____

_________________________ (continue on back, if necessary.)

_____________ _____________ _____________

Signature Title Date

FIGURE 4-1. TDDS Medical Assessment (Form A)

design, crowded and dense. In all fairness to the reporting physician, it must be noted that the requirement of this task is not easy. Doctors are used to describing impairments but are not as comfortable with predicting how such impairments might affect the activities of their patients. Now the new requirement asks for even more—a quantified assessment of that prediction.

Rather than developing a check-list style form, TDDS opted for a relatively open-ended prose report. It is difficult to imagine why such a format was selected in that, given a choice between responding to specific questions and creating a prose response, most people, including physicians, prefer the former. This form requires a task which can seem bothersome and unnecessarily difficult. Not only that, but it also presents information to the bureaucracy in sequences which must then be reordered by that agency to suit its coding needs. In this case, the effort needed to create a prose report is exacerbated by the way the question is presented. That is, the doctors would have to make several passes back and forth to the directions in the form in order to ensure that they have responded fully.

The directions themselves pose an interesting problem. Form A contains four direct directives (using the words, "indicate" and "describe"), and four reports of facts, which function as indirect directives, using the phrases, "should be quantified," "information is needed," "we need to know," and "your report should contain." Here we see the headbumping clash of two centers of bureaucratic authority, the government's and the physician's, both of which are more comfortable with giving directives than taking them. No doubt already resentful of being required to report their findings to the bureaucracy, physicians are even more unlikely to want to be told how to do this. My advice to Legal Services was not to give directives to doctors, who don't like to be told what to do. Giving them directives is likely to be the least productive way to obtain recipient compliance. Doctors are much more responsive to requests for information, for this is consistent with their authoritarian needs.

Grammatically, the second sentence, beginning with "If so," seems to assume a negative interpretation of the first sentence's, "whether your patient's impairment(s) affects their ability to do work-related activities." "Affects" is neither positive nor negative. Thus, the "so" in the following "If so" can only mean something like, "If they do negatively affect such activities." Alternatively, another word, such as "impairs" could be used to replace "affects."

Evidence that the TDDS bureaucracy was at least aware of the authority of physicians is found in the use of personal pronouns. This form manages to personalize the physician-respondent, using "your patient" and "your report," but, at the same time, depersonalizes the patient, using "the" impairments rather than "his" or "her impairments." Perhaps this is not important in a form produced by a physician and submitted to a government bureaucracy, since patients do not see the report and are not likely to be aware of being depersonalized by it. In any case, such depersonalizing of the patient's body is common practice in the medical interview with the patients themselves, justified by some as a way of distancing the doctor from the physically over-intimate situation of the doctor-patient relationship. In a curious way, by using the same language that doctors use with their patients, TDDS may well have been aiding in getting the doctors' compliance here.

Legal Services Revised Form B

Legal Services presented me with two alternative forms to the one then being used in Tennessee, now mandated for revision. The first alternative, here called Form B, is reproduced in its entirety in Figure 4-2.

Form B was obviously an improvement over Form A in terms of document design. There is much more white space on the page, less crowding, and less density. By using the "check the blank" approach, TDDS lets the treating physicians know the things that SSA wants to know, preventing them from including unneeded information and saving everyone precious time. Furthermore, this form sequences the information in a uniform way, making its use by SSA less of a search and match process and easier to code.

With all its improvements, curiously enough, the perspective, or point of view, is still not that of the reporting physician. Rather, it is written from the perspective of the agency. Whereas the doctors talk about "patients," this form specifies "claimants," the bureaucracy's perspective. In fact, the top of the form requests the "patient's" name, but when the form turns to matters of lifting, carrying, walking, standing, and sitting, the "patient" is transformed into a "claimant." One wonders why the "patient" cannot remain a "patient" throughout the form's use.

Perhaps the most significant improvement in Form B is that it requests information rather than giving directives, clearly a strategy more likely to obtain physician compliance. Doctors are used to being asked for information but are unaccustomed to and sometimes even hostile toward being given commands, especially for a task which can easily seem like a nuisance.

The use of asterisks to key the meaning of "occasionally" and "frequently" poses a clutter problem that could be improved by inserting these definitions into the questions themselves.

One suggestion for symmetry and consistency made to improve Form B was to highlight topic headings, creating separate headings for "Other Limitations" and "Medical Findings." Principles of document design indicate that recipient compliance is aided by clear, discrete sectioning. This

Legal Services, Form B
Medical Assessment

Name of patient: ______________________ SSAN ________

Lifting/carrying:
In the course of a regular work day, the claimant can (check one):

____ Lift or carry 50 pounds or more occasionally* to 25 pounds frequently**

____ Lift or carry 20 pounds occasionally* to 10 pounds frequently**

____ Lift or carry 10 pounds frequently**

____ Lift or carry less than 10 pounds only occasionally*

*Occasionally means up to 1/3 of a work day
**Frequently means up to 2/3 of a work day

Walking, Standing, and Sitting:

In the course of a regular work day, the claimant's ability to perform the following activities is (circle the number of hours):

Walking	0	1	2	3	4	5	6	7	8	Unimpaired
Standing	0	1	2	3	4	5	6	7	8	Unimpaired
Sitting	0	1	2	3	4	5	6	7	8	Unimpaired

Please describe any other significant limitations, including postural, manipulative, environmental, or sensory limitations?
What medical findings support any limitations shown above?

Signature of Physician ______________________ Date ________

FIGURE 4-2. TTDS Medical Assessment (Form B)

gives the respondent a sense of continuous progression toward the goal of completing the task, especially when that task might be considered bothersome.

To avoid possible confusion, I also suggested relabeling the "Walking/Standing/Sitting" scales by placing "unimpaired" next to the words they modify, rather than leaving them hanging at the right end of the scale, in order to make it absolutely clear what the numbers 1 to 8 refer to.

There is also a punctuation problem in the sentence beginning "Please

Form B, revised by linguist
Medical Assessment

Name of Patient: ______________________ Soc. Sec. Number: __________

Lifting/Carrying:

In the course of a regular work day, the patient can (please check only one):

_____ Lift or carry 50 pounds or more up to 1/3 of a work day to 25 pounds up to 2/3 of a work day

_____ Lift or carry 20 pounds up to 1/3 of a work day to 10 pounds up to 2/3 of a workday

_____ Lift or carry 10 pounds up to 2/3 of a work day

_____ Lift or carry 10 pounds up to 1/3 of a work day

Walking, Standing, and Sitting:

In the course of a regular work day, the claimant's ability to perform the following activities is (please circle the number of hours):

Walking unimpaired	0	1	2	3	4	5	6	7	8	hours
Standing unimpaired	0	1	2	3	4	5	6	7	8	hours
Sitting unimpaired	0	1	2	3	4	5	6	7	8	hours

Other Limitations:

Are there any other significant limitations, including postural, manipulative, environmental, or sensory limitations? If so, what?

Medical Findings:

What medical findings support any limitations shown above?

Signature of Physician ______________________ Date __________

FIGURE 4-3. **TTDS Form B (Revised)**

describe," which ends with a question mark but is not really a question. I advised that it be converted into a real question, since doctors are more comfortable answering questions than replying to directives.

Finally, I was confused about the meaning of "SSAN" at the top of the form. When I was eventually told that it meant Social Security Number, I suggested that this be made clearer.

My suggested revision of Form B, then is shown in Figure 4-3.

Legal Services, Form C

Medical Assessment of Liability to Do Work-Related Activity

Name of individual Social Security Number

To determine this individual's ability to do work-related activities on a day-to-day basis in a regular work setting, please give us an assessment—BASED ON YOUR EXAMINATION—of how the individual's physical capabilities are affected by impairment(s). Consider the medical history, the chronicity of findings (or lack thereof), and the expected duration of any work-related limitations, but not the individual's age, sex, or work experience.

IT IS IMPORTANT THAT YOU RELATE PARTICULAR MEDICAL FINDINGS TO ANY ASSESSED REDUCTION IN CAPACITY: THE USEFULNESS OF YOUR ASSESSMENT DEPENDS ON THE EXTENT TO WHICH YOU DO THIS.

I. Are LIFTING/CARRYING affected by impairment?

( ) No
( ) Yes

What are the medical findings that support this assessment?

If "yes," how many pounds can the individual lift and/or carry occasionally (from very little up to 1/3 of an 8-hour day)? ____

Frequently (from 1/3 to 2/3 of an 8-hour day) ____

II. Are STANDING/WALKING affected by impairment?

( ) No
( ) Yes

What are the medical findings that support this assessment?

If "yes," how many hours in an 8-hour work day can the individual stand and/or walk; total? ____

without interruption? ____

III. Is SITTING affected by impairment?

( ) No
( ) Yes

What are the medical findings that support this assessment?

If "yes," how many hours in an 8-hour work day can the individual sit; total? ____

without interruption? ____

FIGURE 4-4. TTDS Medical Assessment (Form C)

IV. How often can the individual perform the following POSTURAL ACTIVITIES?

	Frequently	Occasionally	Never
Climb			
Balance			
Stoop			
Crouch			
Kneel			
Crawl			

What are the medical findings that support this assessment?

V. Are the following PHYSICAL FUNCTIONS affected by the impairment?

	No	Yes
Reaching		
Handling		
Feeling		
Pushing/Pulling		
Seeing		
Hearing		
Speaking		

A. How are these physical functions affected?

B. What are the medical findings that support this assessment?

VI. Are there ENVIRONMENTAL RESTRICTIONS caused by the impairment?

	No	Yes
Heights		
Moving Machinery		
Temperature Extremes		
Chemicals		
Dust		
Noise		
Fumes		
Humidity		
Vibration		
Other		

VII. State any other work-related activities which are affected by the impairment, and indicate how the activities are affected. What are the medical findings that support this assessment?

PHYSICIAN'S SIGNATURE ____________________ DATE ______________

FIGURE 4-4. (continued)

Legal Services Revised Form C

The second alternate form (Form C) prepared by Legal Services attempted to get into more detail but, at the same time, appeared more complex and imposing. There is a fine line between how much information is really needed by TDDS and how much information it can hope to get from the treating physician. The items on this two-page form may be easier to answer than those of Form B, but physicians are less likely to be inclined to answer two pages of questions. This Form C alternative is reproduced in its entirety as shown in Figure 4-4.

Although this form is more complete and generally clear in its expectations, one matter of potential ambiguity remains. In II. and in III., the form asks, "without interruption?" It is not clear whether this is a yes/no question or whether the physician is to fill in the blank with number of hours. Assuming that it was a yes/no question, I argued that it would be wise to add "( )yes ( ) no." Likewise, in IV., the terms "frequently" and "occasionally," are undefined. Since earlier forms used the frequencies of ⅔ and ⅓ of a workday, I suggested that these terms might be carried over here as well, if indeed that was what was intended.

Form C manages to avoid directives most of the time, other than in the direction section and in the last, narrative response question about other work-related activities not noted in the preceding questions.

Conclusion

Again, after considerable negotiation, TDDS accepted most of these revisions and produced a form which was satisfactory to Legal Services of Middle Tennessee. Like the National Senior Citizens Law Center, Legal Services performs watch dog services for the general public in an effort to serve consumers and beneficiaries. This case was particularly tricky, since the needs of not one, but two, bureaucratic entities had to be served.

Chapter 5

Bureaucratic Speech: Research on Telephone vs. In-Person Administrative Hearings

Earlier chapters of this book deal with language in the bureaucracy as they were dealt with as a result of court decisions, in actual litigation, or in training that resulted from such litigation. In contrast, this chapter is about bureaucratic language discovered from research. In addition, this chapter deals with spoken language used by a bureaucracy, in contrast with the written language described in the earlier chapters.

Once again, it is the National Senior Citizens Law Center (NSCLC) that brought the impetus to this work. As a result of a court decision in California, NSCLC had access to penalty moneys from an offending corporation to address any significant issue they wanted, as long as it dealt with public communication matters. The Gray Panthers called me for suggestions and I supported the notion of trying to find an answer to the question of the comparative effectiveness of face-to-face administrative hearings versus the increasing tendency of bureaucracies to replace them with hearings done over the telephone.

The explosion of electronic communication in recent decades has proceeded with little or no evaluation of the comparative efficiency of various media, such as the telephone, electronic mail, or teleconferencing, in carrying out bureaucratic tasks such as administrative hearings, especially when compared with the conventional practice of communicating face-to-face. As an outgrowth of this technological explosion, government agencies and businesses have moved rapidly toward voice mail and individual word processors where secretaries and telephone operators formerly held forth. Likewise, bureaucracies that are required by law to conduct administrative hearings for citizens who believe that they have been wronged, have been taking steps to replace face-to-face hearings with telephonic alternatives. They believe that electronic meetings save certain resources, such as travel, meeting space, and time. But other questions have been unasked. For example, is the information obtained through telephonic hearings as accurate, fair, and useful as it is in conventional face-to-face hearings? Are the complainants as comfortable, as forthcoming, as effective or as satisfied in telephonic hearings as they are in the face-to-face setting? Is there something about telephonic communication that affects the potential effectiveness of the complainant? Does the age, gender, or status of the participants play different roles in telephonic versus face-to-face interactions? This study was planned to provide a step toward answers to these questions.

Background

In 1970, the U.S. Supreme Court held that a person's statutory entitlement to welfare benefits cannot be terminated without a predetermination hearing that satisfied the requirements of due process (Goldberg v. Kelly, 397 U.S. 254). Since that time, more and more of the administrative requirements on government agencies have come under due process protection. Goldberg suggested a procedure quite similar to a judicial trial, with testimony, evidence, cross-examination, and the right to counsel. Since that decision, however, the concept of "flexible" due process has also emerged, but staying within the confines of Goldberg's emphasis on personal appearance over, for example, written submissions.

Many, if not most programs involving government benefits, have adopted the oral hearing approach. The degree of formality and procedure varies widely, largely as a way of adjusting to the capability of the beneficiaries. The clear intention throughout was to create a successful and fair hearing.

As the demand for hearings increased and as the funds to support such service diminished, suggestions for modifying the in-person hearing were made. One such suggestion was to make use of the telephone instead of the more costly face-to-face hearing.

This issue is not a new one. In the fall of 1987, Dr. William L. Roper, then chief of the Medicare agency, proposed substituting telephone hearings for face-to-face hearings in most disputes involving Medicare benefits. His proposal met with stiff opposition from members of Congress, attorneys for the elderly, and the Association of Administrative Law Judges, and, as a result, Dr. Roper amended this proposal to make any such telephonic hearings optional and voluntary. One critic of the proposal noted, "Most beneficiaries will not know the advantages of face-to-face hearings and, under pressure from the government, will probably choose phone hearings." (Pear, 8 October 1987) Dr. Roper responded that telephone hearings would speed up decisions on Medicare claims which, at that time, were seriously backlogged.

Dr. Roper's proposal, included in the federal Omnibus Budget Reconciliation Act, section 4037, proposed that the Health Care Financing Administration (HCFA) establish its own hearings and appeals unit to handle Medicare cases, with the projection that administrative law judges handle some fifty percent of the appeals over the telephone. The proposal was not approved by Congress, largely because of congressional concerns about conducting the hearings by telephone rather than in person.

In the General Accounting Office's (GAO) briefing report to congressional committees in April 1988, it was noted: "Assessing that HCFA proposal is difficult because HCFA has not tested its approach and has no empirical evidence to support its key assumptions." In response to this criticism, HCFA officials said, "It would be difficult to test the proposal because . . . it would need to be totally implemented to demonstrate the benefits." Lawrence H. Thompson, the assistant comptroller general, disagreed with HCFA saying, "Testing on a small scale is feasible and should, in our opinion, provide needed information to evaluate HCFA's proposal." (U.S. General Accounting Office, April 1988)

HCFA's proposal to establish its own hearings and appeals unit for Medicare cases, including telephone hearings, has since faded away. On the other hand, the Social Security Administration (SSA) subsequently did away with its field offices. This agency then began to hear all complaints by means of an 800 number telephone system. Insurance carriers currently use both in-person and telephone hearings, leaving the choice to the beneficiary's discretion. Nevertheless, the issue of whether or not hearings can be accurately and effectively accomplished by telephone remained unanswered. It is also possible that HCFA may well renew its initiative for telephone hearings at some future date and that SSA may find a comparison between telephone and in-person hearings instructive.

Toward this end, we proposed research based on two types of data: (1) subjective opinions of a sample of hearing officers and service providers, and (2) objective data from actual tape-recorded face-to-face hearings. NSCLC would carry out an opinion survey and locate tape recordings of actual telephonic hearings for my linguistic analysis. In addition, I would be given access to the names of hearing officers who conduct face-to-face hearings so that I could contact them for permission to accompany them at hearings for my comparison of these with telephonic hearings. The following is a summary of the findings I presented to NSCLC.

Opinion Survey

Forty-one attorneys, paralegals, and service providers responded to a twelve-item questionnaire requesting their opinions about the relative merits of in-person versus telephonic hearings.

Only one of the forty-one respondents expressed preference for telephone hearings over in-person hearings. Nine had no particular opinion, largely because they had never conducted telephonic hearings. Thirty-one respondents expressed a clear preference for in-person hearings.

The one respondent who expressed a preference for telephone hearings must be discussed because he/she reports participating in twenty to thirty such hearings per month, by far the largest representation in this category. This hearing officer reports that the telephone is "much easier for all involved if all issues can be resolved, particularly the negotiation of conditional withdrawals." In short, telephonic hearings are reported to be good for single issues, which have no need for presenting a case, cross-examining, or reviewing documentary evidence.

On the other hand, the majority of respondents who express a preference for in-person hearings cite the following advantages to this method of hearing:

- Conversational repair is easier to accomplish
- Personal appearance of beneficiary is evident
- Evidence of pain or impairment is obvious and visible
- Witness credibility can be assessed
- Communication by means of body language is available and accessible
- Beneficiaries are familiar with the in-person modality
- A live, human being is present
- It is easier to make arguments in-person than over the telephone
- It is easier to review documents when they are in front of both parties at the same place
- The beneficiary's lack of verbal ability (some with limited English) is easier to deal with face-to-face.
- The in-person hearing is better for complex cases

The vast majority who expressed preference for in-person hearings made the following negative observations about telephonic hearings:

- They are awkward—they lack the opportunity for a full presentation of the case
- Administrative law judges cannot evaluate the beneficiary's demeanor and credibility
- Telephonic hearings are more difficult for clients with hearing problems
- Hearing officers cannot access participant's condition visually
- Many beneficiaries are uncomfortable with technology
- Administrative law judges cannot observe the claimants' disability visually
- Arguments are more difficult to make over the telephone
- Reference to documents is difficult by telephone
- It is harder for hearing officers to question beneficiaries who have limited verbal ability or limited English language skills

It is clear from this opinion survey that telephonic hearings were not favored by hearing officers at that time. Of those who had participated in telephonic hearings (not all respondents had), the best that could be said for them was that they could be useful if the case was simple enough.

The opinion survey data, summarized above, outlines some of the real issues that face any decision to use the telephonic hearing as a replacement for or supplement to the conventional face-to-face setting.

Analysis of Actual Hearings

Although it is important to learn the preference of agencies, carriers, and hearing officers, it is even more useful to carry out empirical research on the hearing event itself. Such a study can identify the substantive differences, if any, between the in-person and the telephonic hearing. Following is an analysis of seventeen telephone hearings (by eleven female and six male hearing officers) and eight in-person hearings (all done by male hearing officers).

The sample of hearings analyzed here is not random. For many good reasons, it is not easy to obtain tape-recorded hearings for research purposes. It is equally difficult to obtain permission to observe and tape-record in-person hearings. I am grateful to those who finally agreed to make available the tapes and in-person hearings analyzed here. Although this sample of twenty-five hearings may be considered a convenience sample of relatively small size, it represents twenty-five more hearings than have been analyzed linguistically to date and it provides a baseline for future comparisons. To my knowledge, it provides the only empirical information on this topic.

The telephonic hearings took place in California, Oregon, and Iowa. The in-person hearings took place in Maryland and Virginia. I sat in on all in-person hearings as a non-participating observer and I tape-recorded, with permission, these events. All participants in the study remain anonymous in order to ensure confidentiality.

The following study is a first-level analysis of the strengths and weaknesses of both telephone and in-person hearings on Medicare Part B claims. It is a sociolinguistic analysis, one that analyzes features of language in a social context. Since the hearing is conducted with language and since the hearing is a language event, the methods and theories of linguistics are appropriate here.

Controlled, experimental studies, with large numbers of subjects and statistical measurements, cannot be carried out successfully until first-level, ethnographic and descriptive studies of this type are first accomplished. The reason for this is that studies of the type represented here identify the features that later, more controlled analyses can make use of. In addition, ethnographic and descriptive studies have a value of their own. The linguistic events analyzed are real and they represent the behavior of actual participants. Although the degree to which such studies are considered representative can only be determined by follow-up studies based on random samplings and statistical measurements of significance, there is much to be learned about the behavior of participants from first-level studies.

In the sample of hearings made available for this study, there were four types of participants:

- Hearing officer with beneficiaries
- Hearing officer with physicians
- Hearing officer with service or equipment providers
- Hearing officer with attorneys

Although the focus of this study is on the hearing with beneficiaries, other participant types will also be noted, primarily for contrast. It should be pointed out that only one telephonic hearing involved a service provider and no generalizations will be made from it because of its uniqueness here.

In that this is a sociolinguistic analysis of actual hearings, the variables relevant to such analysis, including age, race, gender, status, income, and occupation, can be correlated with language use. However, because of the extreme confidentiality required here, some of these variables were not made available. There can be no question, however, about the age of the Medicare Part B beneficiaries. Although racial identity was not provided, linguistic evidence makes it clear that all the participants in this study are

Caucasian. Income and occupation data were not made available except as they could be inferred through bits and pieces of conversation in the hearings.

On the other hand, the variables of status and gender were easily transparent in these tape-recorded hearings and these variables are treated in detail throughout the analysis.

Power in the Administrative Hearing

The hearing is one of many types of human communication. People engage actively in different types of communication daily, such as talk between friends or family, or talk between strangers or providers of goods and services. They engage, passively and receptively at least, in more structured communication events such as lectures, classroom discussion, sermons, radio and television newscasts, and entertainment. They engage, somewhat more actively, in doctor-patient communication which, in some ways, is similar to the hearing.

The difference between active and passive communication depends on several conditions. The more equal the participants are in power or status and knowledge, the more active the communication can be; that is, more equality can exist in topic initiation, disagreement, giving directives, and asking questions. The less equal the participants are in power, status, and knowledge, the more the participants with that power, status, and knowledge can dominate in topic introduction, giving directives, and asking questions, among other things.

In an administrative hearing, the hearing officer commonly has the most power, status, and knowledge. The beneficiary is the supplicant, the person who is requesting consideration for real or imagined unfairness of treatment. This means that the beneficiary is in the role of subordinate in this communication event, while the hearing officer is in the superordinate role. There is little or nothing that can be done about the fact that these roles exist. The nature of the hearing event requires them.

The very fact of this role assignment, however, requires certain language strategies of the superordinate hearing officer in order to accomplish the stated objectives of the hearings. The hearing, whether in-person or telephonic, is consistently described by hearing officers as an "informal" effort to bring out relevant facts in the case that might otherwise have been obscured in preceding paper transactions. The degree to which the hearing officer makes the beneficiary as comfortable as possible and reduces the anxiety that tends to hamper the achievement of this goal varies from case to case depending on the skills and personalities of both the hearing officer and the beneficiary. It is not the purpose of this study to suggest ways that participants can improve their communicative interaction, but rather to describe and compare the apparent effects of the two different communicative contexts, the telephonic hearings and the in-person hearings, on the goal achievement and overall efficiency of the hearing process.

Status and Role in Administrative Hearings

Hearings involving attorneys and/or physicians produce quite different status and role relationships than do hearings with beneficiaries. In these hearings, the attorney assumes equal professional status with the hearing officers. On the other hand, physicians in this study gave every evidence of believing that they were of higher status than the hearing officers.

Again, it should be clear that these real or perceived status differences are not the primary focus of this study. Any problems, real or perceived, are with the way our society operates and are not caused by the hearing event. Nevertheless, this status difference can become heightened in the telephonic hearings.

Hearings with Physicians

Prior to one of the in-person hearings, a physician beneficiary telephoned the Medicare office and demanded that a Medical Doctor (MD) in his area of specialization be the hearing officer for this case, since only an MD could possibly understand the medical exigencies involved. This physician was told that this would not be possible and the assigned hearing officer commented that he did not know whether or not the physician would even keep the appointment. When the doctor appeared on schedule, he proceeded to give the hearing officer little tests of his medical knowledge, such as: "Do you know the difference between dependent and independent medical procedures?" When, in his answer, the hearing officer used the carrier's term, "incidental," the physician demanded an explanation of that term. Upon hearing the hearing officer's definition, the physician admitted that it was accurate.

This was a particularly difficult hearing in that the physician put forth his own agenda from the moment the hearing began, constantly interrupting the hearing officer. He began to cooperate more after the hearing officer passed his little test of medical knowledge, and successfully explained that he understood medical concepts and terminology, and, finally, summarized the issues as to whether or not this complex case was assigned or unassigned and how much payment could be allowed the surgeon. From this point on, the physician interrupted less and provided useful information in a clear and systematic way.

This hearing lasted an hour and a half but it was only after an hour that the physician began to listen to the very patient hearing officer's repeated explanations and apparently came to realize that this event was not a war or a test of wills but, rather, a fact-finding session. His perceived status as a physician apparently interfered with his ability to listen to what was being explained.

It is difficult to imagine how this hearing would have been successfully concluded over the telephone. As the physician himself indicated, he would have been interrupted constantly if he had telephoned from his office, adding even more noise to an already difficult communication event. On the telephone, he would not have been able to see the facial expressions reflecting the hearing officer's sympathy, reasoning, and patience. The physician's initial telephone call set the stage for a hostile exchange and he came armed for conflict. Instead of finding an enemy, he found a neutral party, which he at first disbelieved and finally came to accept. During the hearing, the physician read through the entire set of documents provided by the hearing officer, many of which he claimed not to have been given and not to have seen before. This act would have been difficult, if not impossible, in a telephonic hearing.

The other in-person hearings with physicians, although less volatile than the one noted above, support the position that a potential conflict of status between hearing officers and medical professionals is best defused in-person rather than by telephone.

Hearings with Attorneys

The two telephonic and one in-person hearing involving attorneys provides another insight into role and status in hearings. Presumably, the status of attorneys is equal to that of hearing officers (who are often attorneys themselves). Despite the efforts of hearing officers to explain that the hearing is informal and that the rules of evidence do not pertain, attorneys representing beneficiaries in this study tended to present their cases as if they were in court. Hearing officers tended to let them do this if they wanted to, even though this usually extended considerably the length of the hearing. The telephonic hearings with attorneys as representatives were quite adversarial. In both types of hearings, the attorneys gave court-style direct examinations to their own client-beneficiaries. One attorney requested the opportunity to make an opening statement (which was denied by the hearing officer). In contrast, the in-person hearing in which an attorney was present was less adversarial, more informed, but less well sequenced and organized. It should be noted, however, that in this case, his client-beneficiary was the physician who had his own agenda and, quite likely, would not have suffered a direct or cross-examination by anyone, including his own attorney.

The main point to be learned from the presence of attorney-representatives is more general: people are comfortable with the forms of discourse with which they are most familiar. Attorneys are used to the court-style format of opening statements, direct and cross-examination of witnesses, and final arguments. Such an approach offers them the power of language and logic. Medical doctors, as research in doctor-patient communication has shown, are equally concerned about power, but not as much in the exposition of logic as in the power that has been bestowed upon them as unquestionable experts with authority and status exceeding that found in virtually all other aspects of society.

Hearings with Beneficiaries

In stark contrast with the status and power of attorneys and medical doctors is the beneficiary's lack of status and power in the hearings, both in-person and telephonic.

Since most of the hearings in this sample are Medicare Part B, this means that the beneficiaries are elderly people who have been denied their claims and who do not understand why. The superior status and power of the hearing officer is unquestionably assumed in such hearings. In contrast with the hearing events between participants of equal status (attorneys) and with perceived superior status (medical doctors), where the hearing officer's equal or inferior status can hamper effectiveness, in hearings with beneficiaries the hearing officers' innately superior status can also hamper the effort to obtain information. In such cases, hearing officers tried to put the beneficiaries at ease and to assure them of their own neutrality, and that they were only trying to determine the facts that will help them, the beneficiary.

To defuse the asymmetrical status relationship with beneficiaries, the hearing officers carry out six strategies:

1. Rely on informal, conversational style
2. Share (or give up) perceived power

3. Let beneficiary self-generate topics
4. Defuse legal format
5. Take beneficiary's perspective
6. Avoid displays of knowledge

The hearings analyzed in this study evidence a range of success in defusing the asymmetrical status relationship of the beneficiary and the hearing officer. In the telephonic hearings, however, one major difference stands out: the female hearings officers did this much more successfully than did the male hearing officers. In contrast, in the in-person hearings, all of which were conducted, in this study, by male hearing officers, the hearing officers evidenced no such problem. It will become apparent that in this comparison of telephonic and in-person hearings, the variable of gender required careful attention and analysis.

In order to analyze this difference, let us first define and examine these six strategies.

Strategy 1: Rely on Informal, Conversational Style

The concept of register reveals that people shift registers in conversation to accommodate different topics, participants, ages, settings, emotional state, and socioeconomic status. Formal and informal registers differ in such language features as address forms (first name, Ms., sir, Ma'am, etc.), contracted verb forms vs. full forms, presence vs. absence of personal comments (apologizing, thanking, concerns for heath), frequent feedback markers, varied vs. monotone intonation, and the use of indirectness in such potentially negative speech acts as warnings and challenges.

Register shifting is crucial in hearings since beneficiaries are less familiar with the formal register, especially at the required boilerplate beginning phases of the hearing. Beneficiaries cannot be equals with hearing officers in this court-like event, either in procedures or in language. For this reason, it behooves the hearing officer to shift registers effectively at the point in the hearing where it is appropriate, both by permitting or encouraging beneficiaries to use their familiar procedures and language and by using those procedures and language forms themselves, joining the beneficiaries in a neutral search for the facts in the case. It is always the case that, in the search for knowledge, truth, and justice, the powerful are expected to adjust to the powerless, the teacher adjusting to the child, the wealthy adjusting to the poor, the native speaker adjusting to the foreigner. Part of this adjustment is in the language used.

Address Forms

The informal register calls for first name address forms. The formal style calls for Mr., Mrs., Ms., Sir, or Ma'am. In telephonic interviews, where the participants are not present to each other visually, the decision to use the formal or the informal register of address forms is complex. Most people have experienced solicitation phone calls where the soliciting party uses the first name in ways that seem inappropriate (although I have also found that this practice varies by region of the country). The male hearing officers in this sample, when they use any address form at all, use the formal forms (Mr., Sir). It should be noted that male hearing officers use no address form at all to females. Female hearing officers, when addressing female beneficiaries, tend to use first names. To male beneficiaries, female hearing officers use no address form at all unless invited by the beneficiaries to call them by their first name.

Success with the strategy of reducing status asymmetry by using the informal register of first name address forms is accomplished in this sample by only female hearing officers talking with female beneficiaries.

The in-person hearings analyzed here were not different, in this respect, from the telephone hearings.

Contractions vs. Full Forms of Verbs

The informal register calls for the use of contractions rather than the full forms that make for a more formal register. In the telephonic hearings, only one of the male hearing officers consistently used contractions, to the husband representative of a female beneficiary. Female hearing officers used contracted forms frequently and consistently to female beneficiaries but used slightly fewer of them to male beneficiaries.

Success with the strategy of reducing status asymmetry by using contractions in this sample of telephonic hearings was accomplished primarily, but not exclusively, when female hearing officers talked with female beneficiaries.

In contrast with the telephonic hearings, male hearing officers frequently used contracted verbs in the face-to-face hearings.

Personal Comments

The informal conversational register calls for personal comments of various types. The formal register is impersonal. Only one of the male hearing officers in the telephonic hearings made a personal comment to a beneficiary, in this case to a male beneficiary ("I'm glad to hear that you're feeling better"), while female hearing officers consistently made such personal comments both to male and female beneficiaries.

Examples:

Female H.O.:	They're taking good care of you
Female H.O.:	You sound pretty perky
Male H.O.:	I'm glad to hear you're feeling much better
Female H.O.:	Tomorrow's your birthday! Happy birthday to you. Yeah, that's great!

Success with the strategy of shifting register to reduce status asymmetry by making personal comments was accomplished primarily, but not exclusively, by female hearing officers.

The in-person hearings analyzed here, all by male hearing officers, evidenced several personal comments to beneficiaries such as "You have good kids" (spoken to beneficiaries who were being represented at a hearing by one of their adult children).

On the whole, however, the in-person hearings offered fewer personal comments compared with their use by female hearing officers on the telephone. One reason for this may be that males in general simply do not choose to offer personal comments as readily as do females, even when physical contiguity might well be expected to encourage such comments.

Feedback Markers

The informal conversational register calls for frequent use of feedback markers at appropriate places during the speech of the other speaker. This is particularly important in telephone conversations, where the inventory of expressions indicating that one is listening, understanding, and willing to let the speaker continue is limited to audible signals. In face-to-face interactions, however, this inventory extends to many non-verbal signals such as head-nodding, eye-fixation, and smiling and body posture.

Of the various feedback markers, "uh-huh," signals the most informality. "Okay" is also informal, but "right" and "correct" are slightly more formal. The telephonic hearings between male hearing officers and male beneficiaries yielded very few feedback markers of any type, with only one hearing officer using two "uh-huhs" in one hearing. Female hearing officers used a multitude of "uh-huh" feedback markers to female beneficiaries. To male beneficiaries, however, most female hearing officers used the slightly more formal feedback markers "right" and "correct," along with a smattering of "okay." Only one female hearing officer used an abundance of "uh-huh" feedback markers to a male beneficiary.

Success with the strategy of reducing status asymmetry by using informal feedback markers in the telephone hearings was accomplished primarily, but not exclusively, by female hearing officers talking with female beneficiaries. To a slightly lesser extent, such success was accomplished by female hearing officers speaking with male beneficiaries. It was not a very successful strategy for male hearing officers at all, with the exception of one male who often used "okay" with a female beneficiary.

The in-person hearings in this study were carried out only by male hearing officers. Like the males in the telephone hearings, feedback markers were fairly infrequent. The most informal feedback marker, "uh-huh," was rare. More common were "Right," "I understand" or "Okay," consistent with general male speech behavior to males.

Intonation

The informal speech register calls for the intonation patterns of everyday conversation, usually with a wide range of pitch and stress. In the formal register, such variation is reduced and the talk has a more monotone, business-like quality. The male hearing officers clearly used more monotone in the telephone hearings than did the female hearing officers, regardless of the gender of the beneficiary. Success with the strategy of reducing status asymmetry by using varied intonation was accomplished primarily by the female hearing officers.

In contrast, the in-person hearings (male hearing officers to male and female beneficiaries) yielded a range of intonation variability, even in the more formalistic introductory parts.

Directness vs. Indirectness

Another way that informal conversational style is achieved is by using indirectness. Although it is generally believed that being direct in speech is more efficient, clearer, and better than being indirect, this is not always true. Social interaction often requires indirectness for many reasons, including politeness, concern for the other person's feelings, to avoid sounding bossy, or to avoid offending or face-threatening. Directness, on the other hand, appears to be explicit, forthright and useful. Certain aspects of life require as much explicitness as possible, as in the expression of laws, rules, directions, and procedures. Everyday conversation is usually quite different, since there is much more involved than an exchange of information.

The hearing is, at least technically, a legal proceeding. The hearing officer is, at least technically, a judge. The procedure then, at least technically, is one in which directness might be considered advantageous. Hearings that involve professionals, such as physicians or lawyers, place a premium on directness. Non-professional beneficiaries, however, are not used to such directness and are not as comfortable with it. Daily communication, to them, is often less explicit, more inferential, less logical, more polite, and more concerned about the feelings of others, than direct language may permit. Two areas in which the directness/indirectness continuum are relevant are in warnings and challenges.

Mitigated Warnings

Since the hearing grows out of Social Security or Medicare law, it begins with a somewhat formulaic recitation by the hearing officer identifying the participants, the location, how the hearing will be conducted (usually informally), warnings about false statements, the purpose of the hearing, and how a decision will be made. At this point, the hearing officer asks if the beneficiary has received a copy of the file. Finally, the hearing officer recites the known facts in the case and asks the beneficiary whether or not these facts are accurate.

The warnings section of this formulatic opening of the hearing varies greatly in the sample of telephonic hearings analyzed here, ranging from (a) explicit and direct, to (b) mitigated and indirect, to (c) no warning at all (over half of the telephonic hearings in this sample):

Direct warning:

Example 1 (Male Hearing Officer):

> Section 1128.B of the Social Security Act provides for penalties for evidence submitted in the course of a hearing which could be considered as an attempt to gain payment when no payment is due. Example would be altering Medicare records or billing for services not rendered. The penalties are severe, up to a year imprisonment or $10,000 in fines or both if there was anybody convicted for such an offense.

Modified, indirect warning:

Example 2 (Female Hearing Officer):

> Medicare law provides for rather severe penalties for making any statement that you know contains false information although I do not really perceive that happening here.

Example 3 (Male Hearing Officer):

> Federal law provides penalties for making false statements or withholding pertinent evidence.

Although the hearing is a legal proceeding and the hearing officer is required to give the gist of the warning, the tone of the warning can be frightening to the average beneficiary. It is apparent that the warning is more germane to larger financial claims of physicians or suppliers than to the non-professional beneficiary, which is perhaps why it was omitted entirely in more than half of the hearings with beneficiaries. It was the male hearing officers who included either a direct or indirect warning in every hearing while only one hearing conducted by a female hearing officer contained even an indirect warning.

Once again, then, we see a gender difference in the data. Research on gender differences in language shows clearly that females value and use indirectness far more than males and that females are far more sensitive than males to the need for social cooperation and consensus. But does this mean that it is only a female "thing" to omit or modify the warning to be less explicit and direct? Again the answer is no, for three hearings conducted by males used a version of the modified, indirect warnings noted above. It may be the case that female hearing officers are indirect in this regard, but it is equally true that males also can be indirect and therefore, less threatening.

In the in-person hearings with professional and with non-professional beneficiaries, a mitigated, indirect warning was common:

Example 4 (Male Hearing Officer):

> The Medicare law does provide for fines or penalties in the event that any false statements or misrepresentation is of facts are made.

As a warning, this statement fulfills the obligation of the law but it is considerably less threatening than the explicit, direct warning of the telephonic hearing cited earlier. It is less intimidating because it is not as direct as the law ($10,000 fine and/or one year imprisonment). It does not comment on how severe the penalty is, it does not contain the words "convicted" and "offense," and it does not give examples of punishable acts.

Avoid Challenges

Occasionally in a hearing, the beneficiary will give conflicting information to the hearing officer. The direct way to address conflicting information is to challenge with utterances like, "but that's not what you said earlier." However true this may be, such challenges can defeat the intention of obtaining pertinent facts for they put the beneficiary on the defensive.

In one telephonic hearing, the hearing officer read aloud a hospital's report in which the beneficiary indicated that he would have blood drawn at a specific military hospital. Instead, the beneficiary went to the nearest hospital, resulting in a monetary charge that he considered unfair. The hearing officer could have presented this information as a challenge but she didn't. Instead, she said:

> I know that it was a while back and that it is confusing. But I was wondering, she (the writer of the report) says in the last paragraph that his units would be drawn at the (military) hospital.

Here we see an example of an indirect representation of possible conflicting evidence rather than a direct challenge of inconsistency.

In another hearing, the conflict concerned differing definitions of "chairlift" and "seatlift." The beneficiary claimed that his purchase of a chairlift was legitimized by the "Medicare Handbook's" mention of a seatlift chair. The hearing officer does not directly challenge when she says:

> Okay, a seatlift chair is like, I don't know if you've seen them advertised on TV, it is like a recliner that assists you in getting up. The chair lifts up so that it kind of picks up and stands you up. That's what a seatlift chair is.

The hearing officer could have said, directly, "chairlifts (elevators between floors) are not covered but seatlift chairs are." Instead, she defines a seatlift chair, leaving to the beneficiary to see the difference, which he ultimately does.

In another case, the issue grew out of whether an electronic bed was purchased before or after the doctor prescribed it. The female hearing officer presents the issue as follows:

> Now the one thing that I notice is that the bed was purchased, or the date on the invoice that I have is September 8th, and the prescription from the doctor is September 14th. Is there any reason why the prescription is dated after the purchase?

The opportunity for a direct challenge here is obvious, yet the hearing officer avoids challenging by shifting the obvious conflict to her own possible misunderstanding.

In another case involving an electric bed, the beneficiary gives conflicting information. She first says she got the form after she made the purchase, then says she made the purchase after she got the doctor to send in the form. Soon after, she says that the man she purchased the bed from gave her the form to give to the doctor for his prescription. To this conflicting information, the female hearing officer attempts to summarize rather than to challenge the beneficiary's inconsistencies:

> Okay, so I'm understanding you to say that at the time you purchased the semielectric bed, the owner of the company gave you a prescription and the medical necessity form for your physician to fill out. Is that correct?

The adversarial challenge was avoided by the indirectness of a restatement of the most recent story. The hearing is not a matter of winning or losing an argument; it is a matter of getting the facts straight.

In contrast to the indirectness of the above challenges is the hearing in which a beneficiary claimed not to have been sent the file in advance of the telephonic hearing:

> Male Beneficiary: No I don't have your manila folder. I would have saved that if I had it.
>
> Male H.O.: That was attached to the letter. If you got the letter, you got the manila folder, sir.

After considerable fumbling and searching, the beneficiary repeats his claim:

> Male Beneficiary: If it's a file folder, I'll guarantee I didn't get that.
>
> Male H.O.: Well, if you got the letter from me, sir, you had to have gotten that.

There is no indirectness here, no possibility that something might have interfered with the mail processing. The hearing officer stops short of explicitly saying the beneficiary is wrong or even lying, but that inference is unmistakable.

Once again, a major difference can be seen in the way female hearing officers mitigate challenges to conflicting information and the way male hearing officers do not mitigate their challenges, in this sample of telephonic hearings. As noted throughout this study, reducing the asymmetrical status of the participants increased the efficiency and accuracy of the fact-gathering process. In this process, the indirectness of warnings and challenges, both adversarial speech acts, contributes to that goal. Directness does not.

In the face-to-face hearings studied here, the male hearing officers approximated the strategies of the female telephonic hearing officers. In one hearing, the male son representing his aged father (also present) was asked by the male hearing officer about the medical record of his mother. Her claim for oxygen reimbursement had been denied by the carrier. The hearing officer asked:

> I'm curious about one thing. The diagnosis says chronic pulmonary disease. Were any other terms used for this?

The hearing officer could have challenged at this point, for pulmonary disease does not normally signal the use of oxygen on a daily basis. Instead, he shifts the focus to his own lack of understanding of the issue.

In another hearing concerning durable medical supplies, the beneficiaries claimed not to have received an earlier mailed decision from the carrier. The male hearing officer's response contrasts sharply with that of the male telephonic hearing officer cited earlier, involving missing documentation:

> Male Beneficiary: We never got that decision.
>
> Male H.O.: You didn't change your address did you? I just don't know why you didn't get that decision.

Here we have no challenge, as we saw in the telephone hearing. Instead, the in-person hearing officer suggests a possible reason (address change) then leaves the problem unanswered (I don't know why). There was no need to win this contest, since the resolution had little bearing on the matter anyway. The physical presence of the beneficiaries may have contributed to the indirectness of this exchange, but it is also clear that this hearing officer was not combative and was more concerned about resolving the case than winning a battle.

Strategy 2: Share (or give up) Perceived Power

The above analysis points out that the real or perceived status and power of the participants in a hearing is a very important factor in achieving the goal of the hearing, which is to bring out facts relevant to the reconsideration of the preceding denial of the beneficiary's claim. Expression of one's own status and power increases the asymmetrical relationship, telling the other person, in effect, "I am more important than you are and what I have to say matters more than what you have to say." The status and power superiority claims of participating physicians and attorneys can cause the hearing officer to take a defensive stance (although this happened in only one of the telephonic hearings reviewed here), which can give the appearance of non-neutrality. The status and power inferiority of beneficiaries can be self-intimidating, resulting in imperfect, ambiguous, incomplete, or otherwise unsuccessful representation of their facts and knowledge.

The language task of the hearing officers, then, on the one hand, is to tactfully demonstrate their own symmetrical status and power to those such as physicians, who perceive their own status and power to be greater than that of the hearing officer, and, on the other hand, to de-emphasize their own power and status to those who perceive their power and status to be inferior.

The degree to which this language task was accomplished in the sample of telephonic hearings analyzed here has been noted above. It is clear, based on the language features of address forms, contractions, personal comments, feedback markers, intonation, and indirectness, that female hearing officers tended to accomplish this task better than did the male hearing officers in telephonic hearings.

It is also noteworthy that hearings conducted by female hearing officers are shorter in duration than those of male hearing officers. One might hypothesize that by adding personal comments and otherwise being more conversational, these hearings would be longer. But the data indicate that more continuous argumentation, disagreement, and discussion occurs in hearings in which the formal register is established. One can therefore conclude that the deformalizing of the telephonic hearing done consistently by female hearing officers (and by only one of the males) leads to a quicker revelation of pertinent information.

The fact that female hearing officers reduce the asymmetrical relationship of status and power more than male hearing officers does not suggest, however, that males cannot do this well. It indicates only that they generally do not. One need look no further than the current literature on male-female conversational style (see, for example, Tannen 1990), to learn that women are more prone to establishing a social relationship than are men. Indeed, one male hearing officer comes close to the females in this task. The other males, however, are far from such an achievement.

The in-person hearings analyzed in this study point up a number of differences concerning status and power equalization. A male hearing officer met with a male beneficiary and his wife over a denied claim based on differences in the beneficiary's understanding of terms such as "experimental" and/or "investigational" surgical procedures. Although the beneficiary was friendly and polite, a long discussion ensued concerning the carrier's use of these terms. The hearing officer was patient and understanding, offering feedback markers including facial expressions of concern and understanding, head-nods and "uh-huh's" throughout. He varied his intonation appropriately, used contractions, and introduced several comments of a personal nature concerning the well-being of the couple. He did not address the couple by their first names.

Although this hearing could well have produced a heated argument (since the beneficiary was virtually inflamed by the carrier's decision based on what he perceived to be an erroneous use of the disputed terms), the hearing officer patiently and repeatedly explained the conditions involved, in terms that the beneficiary could understand. He established, also through his visible demeanor, that he understood the beneficiary's quandary and even agreed that the carrier denied the claim for the wrong reasons. At issue here was not a great sum of money (some $300) and it became clear that what bothered the beneficiary most was the principle of the matter, not the money. The real issue was fairness and consistency, as the hearing officer realized early in the hearing. He refused to be trapped into a defensive posture and he was extremely tolerant of the beneficiary's many misunderstandings of the process. The hearing concluded with the beneficiary having little hope for any change in his award claim, but he was satisfied when the meeting ended. He had been listened to by a reasonable person. This may have been all that he wanted.

The beneficiary in this case wore a hearing aid and frequently leaned forward to catch what was being said. Visually conscious of this, the hearing officer raised his voice appropriately and repeated himself without being asked. In a telephonic hearing, these visible clues would not be present and the beneficiary would have had to request repetition or clarification many times, a potential face-threatening requirement.

Personal Pronouns

Personal pronoun usage provides clues to the assertion or denial of power and status. The frequency of "I," "my," "me," increases proportionately in these hearings as the hearing officer senses the need to assert power. In the telephonic hearings, female hearing officers use first person singular pronouns primarily in their personal statements, but much less so on topics related to their official role as hearing officer. Male hearing officers, even though they insert far fewer personal statements, use first person singular pronouns more extensively on virtually all topics. The more hearing officers sense the need to control (i.e., with physicians, attorneys, or feisty male beneficiaries), the more "I," "me," and "my" pronouns they use.

Perhaps the most salient aspect of pronoun usage in the hearings grows out of the discussion of its end product, the written decision. It is customary to announce, at the beginning of the hearing, that a written decision will be forthcoming. In all but one of the telephonic hearings, this information was repeated at or near the end of the hearing. In six of the hearings, this decision was also referenced at some point or points after the boilerplate beginning and before the conclusion. The variations used by the hearing officers to convey this information were many, as shown in Figure 5-1:

Although there are no categorical differences in how the hearing officers use personal pronouns in relation to their power as decision makers, the words, "my decision," were used thirteen times by the six male hearing officers but only four times by eleven female hearing officers. Males did not use this term to female beneficiaries. A female hearing officer used the term to only one male beneficiary. Only one of the female hearing officers

Placement introduction:	Male H.O.	Female H.O.
My decision will be in writing	3	1
I will make an independent decision in writing	3	7
(No mention of decision)	0	3
Middle:		
(No mention of decision)	3	8
A decision	1	0
I'll write my decision	2	0
I'll write a decision	0	1
I'll take all that into consideration	0	1
Conclusion:		
I'll send my decision	1	2
I'll get this/that decision out to you	1	2
I'll send a/the decision	3	0
The decision will be in writing	0	1
You'll receive a letter	0	2
You'll be receiving my correspondence	0	1
We'll get back to you as quickly as we can	0	1
(No mention of decision)	1	1

FIGURE 5-1. Personal Pronouns Used by Hearing Officers

used the term at all to female beneficiaries. This suggests strongly that the power assertion, so heavily present in the authoritative words, "my decision," is favored by males when talking with male beneficiaries.

The female hearing officers' preferred strategy for the concluding reference to the ultimate written decision is to replace "my decision" with "the decision" or "that decision," distancing themselves slightly from the personal pronoun, or to avoid the word "decision" altogether, replacing it with "letter," "correspondence," or "I'll get back with you."

The female hearing officers' preferred strategy for the introductory reference to the ultimate written decision is the formulaic "I will make an independent decision in writing," whereas the male hearing officers split evenly between the same formulaic expression and "My decision will be in writing." The formulaic version is, itself, somewhat mitigating, including as it does the word "independent" and converting the act into a process ("I will make") rather than a static entity ("my decision").

Once again, it is clear that the gender difference is not categorical. Males can avoid the power asymmetry so evident in the personal pronoun attachment in "my decision." The fact is that they tend not to, whereas females avoid it more systematically.

In the face-to-face hearings, the male hearing officer's personal pronoun referencing approximated that of the female officers in the telephonic hearings. When referring to the written decision that would result from the hearing, there were no instances in which the possessive pronoun *my* appeared contiguously with *decision*. The consistent references to that decision were the following:

- The decision that I will send out to you . . .
- I'll make a written decision . . .
- I'll make an independent decision . . .
- The letter will be out in three weeks or so. It will contain the decision, my reason for it, and the appeal rights.

Once again, the in-person hearings evidence a relinquishing of perceived power, this time by depersonalizing the written decision (i.e., a decision, an independent decision, the letter, the decision) by separating the personal pronoun from the word, "decision," and by defining the hearing officer's role as agent of the process rather than owner of the decision itself.

Winning or Losing

Another indisputable aspect of power involves winning rather than losing. The following excerpts from telephonic hearings illustrate how a hearing officer gave up the need to win in order to equalize footing with the beneficiary:

Example 1:

Female H.O.: I'm not trying to argue. Maybe I don't understand what you're saying.

Male Beneficiary: I'll keep quiet and let you—

Female H.O.: No, you're doing just fine, Mr. X.

Example 2:

Female H.O.: And I can certainly appreciate your point that you've done everything that you could to find out what the guidelines were and to adhere to them . . .

Example 3:

Male H.O.: . . . I just wanted to let you know that no one is trying to say that the oxygen wasn't medically necessary for you.

Example 4:

Female Beneficiary: That's a mistake.

Female H.O.: Most definitely . . . I do need to correct that.

The hearing officers in these sample passages give clear indication that they are not there to win an argument, defend a mistake, or challenge the needs of the beneficiaries. A power move would have been to win the argument, justify the mistake, and ignore or defuse the beneficiary's needs. Most hearing officers did not assert their power in this way. Those who chose to assert their power and status, however, provide instructive contrasts in language use, as the following examples illustrate:

Example 1:

Male Attorney for Beneficiary: . . . the employment division is required by law to communicate to a claimant in a language which the claimant can understand.

Male H.O.: Give me a cite, Mr. X . . . are you going to recite a federal statute?

(after further exchanges)

Male H.O.: . . . all I wanted you to do was give me a cite. You said that law requires it. I wanted you to give a cite of the law you are talking about.

Example 2:

Male Attorney for Beneficiary: I would ask for the opportunity to submit a written statement, since you don't want me to give my full statement orally.

Male H.O.: What do you mean, I don't want your full statement orally?

Male Attorney for Beneficiary: You told me to move it along.

Male H.O.: I didn't tell you I didn't want your full statement.

In all, the above hearing contained eight challenges that indicate the need to win an argument or a point. Four were made by the hearing officer and four by the representing attorney. This hearing proceeded much like a trial with direct and cross-examination of several witnesses, swearing in of witnesses, objections, and opening statements (curiously enough, the hearing officer precluded closing statements).

Although it has been the custom of such hearings to let the beneficiaries present their case in any form they choose, including being represented by an attorney, the hearing described above suggests that the courtroom-style of hearing works against the professed goal of letting beneficiaries present any new information or explanation of already existing facts that might assist their case. Once the format of a trial is selected, the speech event can easily become adversarial rather than cooperative, as this hearing provides clear evidence. Winning takes precedence over all else. Challenging becomes the norm, not the exception. Beneficiaries do not self-generate their positions. The hearing officer, almost by definition and certainly by instinct, assumes power and status above all others. The beneficiary's perspective is severely limited. In short, a courtroom style discourages the hearing officer from using the very language strategies shown in this study to be effective stimulants of beneficiary openness, such as conversational style features, sharing of power, and self-generated statements.

In the face-to-face hearings studies here, the male hearing officers gave no evidence of the need to win the argument, defend a mistake, or challenge the beneficiary.

Strategy 3: Letting the Beneficiaries Self-Generate Topics

It is a well-known fact in fields in which interrogations occur that the most valuable type of exchange is one in which the answer is least influenced by the question. Certain types of questions influence answers more than others, challenging the accuracy of whatever is being measured (as in classrooms) or the truthfulness of the response (as in police interrogation). The greatest accuracy and truth value comes when the response is most self-generated, not influenced by the questioner. Tag-questions are the most suggestive, for they invite (even script) the expected answer ("You were there, weren't you?"). Yes-no and choice questions are also influential, for they reduce the field of possible answers to two, often eliminating important information that cannot be embodied in a simple yes or no. "Why" questions narrow the field of answers somewhat but they allow for multiple possibilities. Open-ended questions are clearly the preferred type for self-generated answers, since they limit the respondent the least. The major argument against open-ended questions is that of time and efficiency. Respondents may ramble and take up valuable time.

It is clear that in hearings of the type examined here, the open-ended beginning is highly valued. In all but one of these hearings, the hearing officer, after completing the formulaic, required beginning format, opened the floor to the beneficiaries to proceed as they saw fit. This was equally the case in telephonic and in-person hearings. The sole instance of violation was one telephonic hearing in which a male hearing officer asked five questions before opening the floor to the beneficiary.

One major difference exists, however, in the types of open-ended questions formed in the telephonic hearings. Every male hearing officer focused the open-ended question by saying, "tell me why you disagree with the denial." Only one female hearing officer focused the open-ended question in this way. Their questions are illustrated as follows:

- Tell me anything that you would like to help me make a decision in your favor.
- I will give you the floor and you go on into what it is you wish to give me.
- Would you like to discuss this with me and tell me what your feelings are on this or your understanding of this.

These questions are clearly broader than "why you disagree," allowing more leeway of response, offering the dignity of self-generation, and avoiding the face-threatening act of interrogation. They also admit the possibility that the issue was more than a disagreement about the amount of money allowed by the carrier. Indeed, an in-person hearing officer reported that he regularly discovers that the major issue is often not about money at all. It is about being listened to, being understood, being treated fairly, and getting clear answers about why claims were denied.

Strategy 4: Defusing the Legal Format

As noted earlier, the formal format of a legal proceeding emphasizes the asymmetry of power in the social relationship between hearing officer and beneficiary. It is a language event that is largely unknown to the average beneficiary, and one which easily leads to tenseness, defensiveness, and argumentiveness.

It was noted earlier that, technically at least, the hearing is, by definition, a legal proceeding. Guidelines have attempted to ensure, however, that not all aspects of a legal proceeding are followed. Most hearing officers state that the proceeding will be conducted "in an informal manner" and that "the usual rules of evidence do not apply." On the other hand, the structural framework of the hearing has many of the characteristics of a legal procedure. This structure can be described, in fact, as a thirteen-phase procedure:

Phase	*Register*	*Example*
1. Opening	formal	The hearing is now opened . . .
2. Identification	formal	Services were provided to Mr. X . . . The control number assigned is . . . My name is . . .
3. Disclaimer	formal	I do not represent the carrier or its position in the matter.
4. Manner	formal	The usual rules of evidence do not apply.
5. Purpose	formal	You will have the opportunity to present testimony and evidence, and the proceeding will be tape-recorded.
6. Product	formal	Following the hearing I will make an independent decision based on the record . . . within thirty days of the close of the hearing.
7. Involvement	formal	The first knowledge I had of this case was when . . .
8. Document check	formal	I sent you a copy of the file. Have you received it?

9. State facts	formal	I will begin by stating the facts and issues of the case.
10. Request for beneficiary's position	less formal	Why don't you go ahead and tell me why you disagree with the denial.
11. Body of hearing	informal	(Led by beneficiary)
12. Product	formal	I will issue a decision in writing.
13. Closing	formal	Thank you very much. This hearing is now closed.

It is, indeed, something of a paradox that a hearing can start and end formally, yet develop a certain informality in phases ten and eleven, the parts of the hearing that consume the most time and contain the salient information and discussion. The extent to which hearing officers begin in a court-like matter yet engineer a switch to a conversational register is the focus of this section.

As noted earlier, part of the hearing officers' success in defusing the legal format is found in how they handle phase ten, "Request for beneficiary's position." Some examples of verbal strategies that seemed to work are the following:

Examples:

1. Okay, now I will turn it over to you and you can add what you would like.
2. Okay, why don't you tell me at this point why you disagree with the amount that was allowed and what you *feel* the amount should be? Or whatever you have.
3. And now at this point Mr. X, I will let you tell me anything that you would like to help me make a decision in your favor.
4. Okay, then I will give you the floor and you go on into what it is you wish to, you know, the information you wish to give me.
5. Ah, would you like to discuss this with me and tell me what your feelings are on this or your, uh, understanding of this?

As noted earlier, the requests for the beneficiary's position are very open ended. Even Example 2, which asks why there is disagreement, mitigates this focus with "or whatever you have." Two of the examples use the word "feel" or "feelings," quite the opposite of a formal court proceeding which seeks only facts. Four of the five examples begin with pause fillers, "Okay" and "Ah," adding a non-formal touch to the previous more formulaic talk. One example contains a very casual, "you know," in mid sentence.

The in-person hearings examined here contained much the same features at this phase of the hearing. In addition, however, non-verbal cues underlined the switch from formal to informal register. The hearing officer smiled, relaxed visibly, leaned back, and gestured in a friendly way to the beneficiary. There was a noticeable change in tone from this point on, even with two physician beneficiaries, and most certainly with the lay beneficiaries.

Not all of the hearings managed the defusing of the legal format that well. In one telephonic hearing, the first five minutes of conversation consisted of a rather pointed exchange about whether or not the beneficiary had indeed received the documents that the hearing officer claimed had been sent. The volatility of this exchange resulted in the maintenance of a formal, legal tone which the hearing officer never abandoned. He used formal address forms (including "Sir") and no contractions or feedback markers. He mentioned his decision sixteen times during the hearings, twelve of which were preceded by "my." He made frequent use of legal or technical terms even after the formulaic introduction, including "stipulate," "precedent," "comply," "compliance," "sanctions," "ancillary services," "liability," "waived," "testify," "legal rights," "secondary insurance," "liable," and "maintain the integrity of the correspondence."

In another hearing, the one mentioned earlier, which did not begin with an open-ended question that could allow the beneficiary to tell her story first, the legal format was maintained with a series of five questions from the hearing officer. At this point, the hearing officer said: "These are the only questions I had. If you have testimony that you would like to present in your case, you can proceed." In contrast with the expressions used by other hearing officers, this hearing officer used legal register terms such as "testimony," "present," "case," and "proceed."

One of the two telephonic hearings in which an attorney represented the beneficiaries was lawyerly and formal in tone throughout, as might be expected. The hearing officer requested citations of case law and used terms such as "let the record reflect," "going off the record," "receive testimony," "I've marked that document as Exhibit 5," "questions for this witness," and many others. Witnesses were put under oath, attorneys made courtroom-style objections, and the hearing officer made rulings on them.

In all fairness, it should be pointed out that the other telephonic hearing involving an attorney who represented a beneficiary was considerably more informal in tone. Once the formulaic introduction was completed, the hearing officer turned things over to the attorney-representative, saying "You can proceed with whatever line you're going to take." The attorney then began asking his client questions. When the beneficiary described his awful accident, the hearing officer responded sympathetically, "good grief." He maintained this non-legal tone throughout, offering frequent feedback markers and responding "you bet" to the attorney's request to make a brief argument about the regulations in the informal register.

The in-person hearings involving attorneys were much like the latter example. If the attorney chose to sound legal, the hearing officer permitted it but did not, himself, adopt the legal format. Once again, it should be noted that the in-person hearings had the advantage of visual context to support the hearing officer's goals. Smiling, gestures, body postures, and even seating alignments contributed to the reduction of legal format formality in ways that were usually not available in the telephonic hearings.

Strategy 5: Taking the Beneficiary's Perspective

The field of rhetoric considers one of the desirable characteristics of effective communication to be an ability to take the perspective of the reader or listener, called recipient design. Pedagogy has long argued that good teaching begins with learners where they are. This principle is equally inescapable in the hearings analyzed here. If it is agreed that the goal of the hearing is to give the beneficiaries the opportunity to present evidence to support a decision in their favor, as several hearing officers put it, then it is obvious that the hearing officer should do everything possible to help the beneficiary bring out that perspective. Without overlooking the facts, the law, or regulations, the hearing officer must also try to see things from the beneficiary's perspective. Part of achieving the beneficiary's perspective is accomplished through the features described above: relying on conversational style, sharing power, allowing self-generated talk, and defusing the legal format. In addition, however, there are several other ways that the beneficiary's perspective can be brought forth.

It was noted earlier that certain speech acts are, by definition, face-threatening and negative. Warnings and challenges were analyzed as face-threatening speech acts in these hearings. These, along with threatening, complaining, and denying, constitute the most negative types of language functions. On the other hand, the speech acts of thanking, promising, praising, agreeing, offering, congratulating, sympathizing, and certain types of admitting, provide positive affect in communication and are generally perceived to indicate that those who generate these speech acts are at least friendly to the listener's cause and are receptive to the beneficiary's perspective. Most examples of these speech acts can be regarded as simple expressions of social politeness. Following the pattern noted throughout this study, in telephonic hearings, female hearing officers gave evidence of taking the beneficiary's perspective far more commonly than did male hearing officers. All but two female hearing officers gave such evidence but only one male did so.

Examples of statements in which the hearing officer's speech acts successfully took the perspective of the beneficiary are the following:

- I can actually appreciate your point that you've done everything that you could to find out what the guidelines were and to adhere to them.
- Sometimes that's the only route that you do have open, is to do this (ask for a hearing).
- I'm glad to hear you're feeling much better.
- You feel that your doctor prescribed it and that since he prescribed it to you, who know your condition better than your doctor, . . .
- Tomorrow's your birthday! Happy birthday to you, that's great.
- You're doing fine, Mr. X.
- It was nice speaking with you on the phone. I appreciate your taking the time to speak with me.
- I will check on that and make sure that you get one.

One-third of the telephonic hearings contained no evidence at all of taking the beneficiary's perspective. In contrast, the in-person hearings evidenced a multitude of speech acts that evidence the hearing officer's appreciation for the beneficiary's perspective. One reason for this is found in the fact that it is much more difficult to be face-threatening or confrontational face-to-face than it is when the participants are present only to each other's voices. The more physical distance separating participants, the easier it is to confront, largely because of the cooperative principle that makes conversation work. It is a well-recognized fact that written language, such as memos or letters, can be even more face-threatening, critical, or confrontational than telephonic conversation.

The closer the physical relationship, the more confrontation is defused, as Figure 5-2 illustrates.

It is clear from the evidence in this sample of hearings that face-to-face hearings reduce or defuse existing confrontational characteristics far better than do telephonic hearings. The reason for this is found in the long-understood fact that physical contiguity encourages taking the other person's perspective.

	face to face	telephone	written
high			•
mid		•	
low	•		

FIGURE 5-2. Frequency of Negative Face Threatening and Confrontation Across Cummunicative Modes

Strategy 6: Avoiding Displays of Knowledge

To physicians, the hearing officers' task is often to convince the doctor that they know enough to assess the complex medical situation in dispute. We have already noted how some physicians demand such knowledge, while attorney-representatives of beneficiaries appear to presume somewhat equal knowledge on the part of hearing officers. On the other hand, beneficiaries presume knowledge and power of the hearing officer far beyond their own. As we have seen, such a presumption, whether true or false, helps create an asymmetrical social relationship which has great potential for impeding the accuracy and efficiency of the exchange. For example, if the beneficiary believes or suspects that the other, more knowing, participant already knows everything, then there seems to be no reason to tell him or her what that beneficiary knows. To a presumed all-knowing person, one often runs the risk of appearing ignorant or foolish by saying anything at all.

To defuse this role of all-knowingness, hearing officers have the option of revealing their own vulnerability. Strategies for accomplishing this include the following:

1. Stressing their interpretation of evidence rather than the indisputable truth of it.

   Examples:

   - facts and issues of the case as I interpret these as I understand the issues

2. Admitting their lack of knowledge.

   Examples:

   - I don't know how to pronounce it . . .
   - I can't really tell if this is an invoice . . .
   - I'm not exactly sure what the geographical area is . . .

3. Admitting their failure to understand.

   Examples:

   - I was basically wondering . . .
   - Well, one thing I noticed was . . .
   - I don't understand why there wasn't a customary rate established.

As the examples above constitute the entire body of vulnerability statements made by all hearing officers in the telephonic hearings studied here, it is clear that this strategy was not especially favored. Two females and one male hearing officer produced all seven instances.

A more salient measure of how hearing officers avoided displays of knowledge may be found in what they could have said but chose not to say. It is admittedly difficult to discuss what was not said, since no concrete evidence of this exists. What can be done, however, is to point out cases in which more information was given than was required, as touchstones for the absence of such information given by other hearing officers.

Again, only the hearings with lay beneficiaries were examined, since the verbal strategy for dealing with physicians and attorney-representatives, as noted earlier, calls for a quite difference approach.

One maxim of the cooperative principle of conversation, "make your contributions as informative as required, not more so," is the issue here. Only two telephonic hearings with lay beneficiaries violated this maxim. The following example illustrates one of them:

> Male H.O: Okay, what I'm saying then is the maximum allowable actual charge is an amount that is arrived at by using a calculation of the previous, they use a calculation of the prevailing charge to develop the max, and what the max is for non par-Medicare has participating and non-participating physicians now, participating is where they agree to accept Medicare assignment for all the claims to all their patients. That means they agree to accept the full Medicare allowed charge minus the 20% co-insurance and deductible, while non-participating they do not have to accept assignment on any claims. They can if they want on an individual basis but they're not obligated to accept assignment, but in order to help, you see the cost was still going up and the Medicare beneficiaries like yourself were then responsible for the entire charge to the physician, so in order to try and cut the amount of cost that the beneficiaries were responsible to, to the physicians, the Medicare law or law was passed where there's a cap that was put on the amount that a physician could charge to a patient for a particular service under Medicare. And that's called the Medicare allowable actual charge, so for the one procedure you have underlined on that sheet, which is not the same procedure that was performed but it is close, is 25575, which is open treatment for radial end ulna

> OK, the fee screen 1990 max charge was $1,581.72, OK, that's the maximum amount that that physician can charge when he's billing a Medicare patient for that service. OK, but the prevailing OK, now when you are talking about how much Medicare will allow, OK, Medicare allows the lowest of the billed amount. OK, the physician customary charge for that service, it's not during the same year that he's charging for those, it's during the fee screen in that data period that we collect the charges for that fee screen year. An example of what I'm telling you is that for service that was rendered in fee screen 89, OK, that's January 1 through December 31 of '89, the period of time that we collect the data to develop the profile is from July 1, 1987 through June 30, 1988. OK, well, so the customary charges developed by charges that the physician makes for the service during the data collection period, this is his customary charge. We then look at other physicians of the same specialty performing the same service during the same period of time and that is determined to be the prevailing charge. OK?

Another salient example of a hearing officer displaying more knowledge than necessary is also given by another male telephonic hearing officer. The male beneficiary had complained throughout about not being able to understand various aspects of Medicare law. At one point, the following exchange took place:

> Male H.O.: . . . As far as the requirements for law on the amount in controversy, I will be happy to research the code of federal regulations and send you the citation verbatim. I'll quote it for you.
>
> Beneficiary: I would appreciate just for peace of mind. I'm not an attorney and may not understand when I see it.
>
> Male H.O.: It's very simple to understand. It's written in such a way that if you stop and read it, it's simple to understand . . . There are not very many physicians that understand this either until this is brought to their attention.

In this somewhat condescending explanation, the hearing officer establishes that he has no trouble understanding something that most physicians find confusing. For him, at least, the code is quite simple.

In contrast, the in-person hearings analyzed here revealed no instances of hearing officers displaying more information than was required and there are no displays of such personal knowledge.

Advantages and Disadvantages of the Hearing Formats

From the analysis of actual hearings carried out in this study, it is apparent that telephonic hearings can elicit accurate and useful information for a hearing officer's fair decision if the case is not complex, if the beneficiary is able to hear and communicate effectively, if both the beneficiary and the hearing officer are well prepared and organized at the time of the call, if the telephone modality does not intimidate the beneficiary, and if the beneficiary and hearing officer can overcome unfamiliarity and/or discomfort with the asymmetry in social role and power which is inherent in such events. If such handicaps can be overcome, the telephone hearing can accomplish at least some of the economic savings predicted by the Medicare agency in 1987.

On the basis of the hearings analyzed in this study, it would appear that many hearings involving physicians might be economically and accurately accomplished by telephone. Physicians claim to have severe time problems, tend to have more complete written records, and seem to be able to articulate their positions more effectively than beneficiaries. Even so, however, complex cases involving large amounts of paperwork which must be discussed seem better suited to face-to-face hearings. In such cases, physicians, by their own admission, benefit from being away from the constant demands and distractions found in their offices, even when they are in a telephone call hearing.

The extent to which telephone hearings can be considered as effective, fair, accurate, and useful in cases involving attorney-representatives of beneficiaries is less clear from the sample hearings analyzed in this study. One telephone hearing worked rather well; another was consistently confrontational, slow, and complex. The single in-person hearing involving an attorney was more difficult to assess because it also contained a physician and evidenced conflicting agendas that were not always made explicit. Once again, based on the few hearings studied here, it appears that the telephonic hearing involving attorney-representatives can accomplish at least some of the economic savings predicted by the Medicare agency in 1987 if the case is not complex, if both the attorney and the hearing officer are well prepared and organized at the time of the call, and if the attorney's more comfortable predisposition to the procedures of a courtroom can be effectively accommodated or adjusted.

The main focus of this study, however, is with lay beneficiaries. It is this focus that provides the more salient areas of comparison between telephone and in-person hearings. Most crucial indicators are the degree to which hearing officers switch from the formal to the informal register, use conversational style, share or give up their perceived power, permit the beneficiary to self-generate, defuse the legal format, take the beneficiary's perspective, and avoid displays of knowledge.

Switching from Formal to Informal Register

This strategy, being closely associated with the leveling of asymmetrical power, has the potential for being more effectively accomplished face-to-face than by telephone, simply because the inventory of features to accomplish it is greater in face-to-face settings. That is, all of the language features are available in the face-to-face setting plus all of the non-verbal features such as body movement, facial expression, eye-gaze, gesturing, seating arrangement, and head-nodding, all evidence of attentiveness, understanding, or perplexity.

The hearing is composed of more than verbal language. It is social interaction as well. As it turns out, most female hearing officers accomplished this switch far better than did most male hearing officers. It should be pointed out that the original intent of this study was not focused on gender differences. But since the use of aspects of conversational style salient to the accomplishment of a social relationship are more generally common among females than males, the gender factor surfaced quite naturally. This was particularly evident in the use of feedback markers, personal comments, varied intonation, contractions, indirectness, and informal address forms, all far more commonly realized by female than male hearing officers. On the other hand, in the face-to-face hearings, male hearing officers produced a far greater frequency of these features than male hearing officers produced in the telephone hearings, suggesting strongly that face-to-face communication generates more relational social interaction than does the less personal, formal hearing style conducted more commonly by males. This being the case, the in-person hearing can be said to more successfully establish the informal register which, in turn, contributes to the reduction in asymmetry of social role and power.

Sharing or Giving Up Perceived Power

This study found that the degree to which it is necessary to share or give up perceived power depends almost entirely on the status of the participants in the hearing. With physicians, it is necessary for hearing officers to try to establish equal status and power. In contrast, with beneficiaries it was necessary to give up or share perceived power in order to encourage the kind of communication that can most effectively reveal the salient facts in the case. How this was done also depended, to a large extent, on the participants themselves. Female hearing officers more readily and consistently shared or surrendered power than did male hearing officers, probably as a result of the conventional female perception of communication as the establishment of a social relationship. Again it should be emphasized that this gender difference is not categorically realized, since a minority of male hearing officers also shared or gave up perceived power to beneficiaries and a minority of female hearing officers did not. The central finding of this aspect of the study, however, is that male hearing officers in the in-person hearings gave up perceived power in degrees approximating the extent that female hearing officers did so in telephonic hearings.

This study points out how the use of personal pronouns, especially contiguous to the word, "decision" (i.e., my decision), occur primarily in telephone hearings. A second finding concerns the sheer quantity of first person singular pronouns per hearing: the more such pronouns are used, the more power is being asserted and, consequently, the more confrontational the event becomes. Again, female hearing officers use such personal pronouns far less frequently than do males. In the face-to-face hearings observed in this study, male hearing officers used relatively few first person singular pronouns overall and, when they did, they tended to put distance between it and the word, "decision" (i.e., "I will make an independent decision"), following a common pattern of female hearing officers in the telephone hearings. One can reasonably conclude from this that the physical closeness between participants discourages confrontation, face-threatening, and even more indirect assertions of power (see Figure 5-1).

Once it is clear that the hearing officer has surrendered status and power through the use of the informal register and the mitigation of first person singular pronoun usage, it is easy enough to track other evidence of the hearing officers' efforts to avoid the trap of winning vs. losing an argument. This usually comes in the form of passing up easily winnable inconsistencies in beneficiary statements or in passing up opportunities to justify one's own (or Medicare's) behavior.

Letting the Beneficiaries Self-Generate Topics

This study finds that virtually all hearing officers, whether in telephonic or in-person hearings, arrived at a point in the hearing when they asked the beneficiaries to self-generate, to tell their story in whatever way they wanted to tell it. Nevertheless, a major difference in how this was accomplished in the telephone hearings is found between female and male hearing officers. Males asked beneficiaries why they disagreed with the denial, while females chose to be less focused on the beneficiary's reasons for disagreement. The male hearing officers in the face-to-face hearings studied here followed the broader pattern of the female telephonic hearing officers, suggesting, once again, that the closer the physical participation, the more the hearing officers downplay disagreement, confrontation, and face-threatening interrogation, even in so desirable a characteristic as permitting the beneficiaries to self-generate topics rather than respond to a series of questions.

Defusing the Legal Format

Once the opening formalities are completed, hearing officers tended to let the beneficiaries proceed in whatever manner they chose. If an attorney representative wished to follow a courtroom direct and cross-examination format, hearing officers seldom objected. In the hearings analyzed here, only one hearing contained anything like a courtroom format, even when attorneys participated.

A more serious problem is created by the apparent belief of hearing officers that they must use a legal-sounding, boilerplate register during the first nine phases of the hearing, from the opening to the statement of facts in the case. Telephonic and in-person hearing officers alike moved rapidly and monotonously through these phases, as through reading from a prepared script. It gives the impression that this part of the hearing is something to be endured, to be put on the record, and to get over with as soon as possible. Beneficiaries sat silently and somewhat nervously during this part.

If phases one through nine could be recast into more informal, less legal-sounding, conversational language, the burden of defusing it would be less difficult. As it exists now, however, this part of the hearing is reminiscent of reading the Miranda warnings to a suspect in a criminal case.

The task of overcoming the legal-format tone in order to set beneficiaries at ease so as to effectively present their information is made more difficult than it needs to be by the extant procedure of both telephone and face-to-face hearings. As noted in this study, male hearing officers in the telephone hearings tend to focus on the dispute (i.e., "tell me why you disagree") and ask for a reasoned explanation. Female hearing officers take a broader perspective (i.e., "tell me anything you want") and ask for the beneficiaries' feelings or understandings of the matter.

The in-person hearings, all with male hearing officers, came close to the strategies of the female hearing officers who used the telephone, suggesting, once again, for males at least, that as physical distance between participants decreases, so does the apparent need to be confrontational.

There appears to be no way to defuse the legal format in hearings for which attorneys request a court-like procedure. Once this die is cast, there is no way out. Beneficiaries who ask attorneys to represent them may well, in fact, have to expect this.

Taking the Beneficiary's Perspective

All of the hearings analyzed here make it clear that the hearing officers do not represent Medicare or the carrier and that they are neutral and independent agents appointed to resolve the issue. In no case was there any reason to doubt their objectivity about the resolution of the issue, although some (particularly male) hearing officers were less than objective in their relationship with the beneficiaries. That is, while possibly maintaining their neutrality about the decision, they still competed with the reasoning of the client. The need to win, even while being neutral, remains very strong in human beings, especially males.

Interestingly enough, in phase nine of the hearing, the hearing officer presents what is essentially the carrier's perspective on the issue. Having done this, it is next necessary to get the beneficiary's perspective. This is not merely a matter of cold reasoning. The beneficiaries' perspective may be that they simply do not understand what Medicare or the carrier has told them. For example, one in-person hearing beneficiary complained: "They gave me a denial with nothing in it that I could comprehend as a reason . . . I'm still looking for the first lucid explanation."

It is curious that a third of the telephone hearings studied here contained no evidence of taking the beneficiary's perspective. One can speculate that this grows out of an overly conscientious effort to appear neutral. If so, one wonders why the carrier's perspective can be clearly articulated while the beneficiary's is not. Do some hearing officers see their task as explaining only one side of the dispute? If so, their claims of neutrality are hollow. A more likely explanation is that hearing officers who fail to take the beneficiary's perspective simply either did not have the conversational skills to do so or were not inclined to use them. Once again, the traditional predisposition of females to see conversation as a relationship rather than as a contest puts female hearing officers at an advantage over males. It is primarily the male hearing officers in the telephone hearings that fail to determine the beneficiary's perspective.

The in-person hearings, however, are a different matter. One male hearing officer sensed early on that the reason why the beneficiary asked for a hearing concerned the fairness of Medicare policy. Since Medicare policy is not the purpose of the hearing, the hearing officer did all that he could to explain the procedures the beneficiary should follow to make his case in the appropriate forum, meanwhile sympathizing with this position and quite clearly understanding it. There were no challenges, no criticisms, no efforts to win an argument, no attempts at justification of the decision, the carrier, or Medicare policy. The hearing officer took the beneficiary's perspective and was engaged primarily in helping him resolve it.

Taking the beneficiary's perspective includes direct, performative statements which express appreciation of the beneficiary's perspective, concern for the beneficiary's well-being, and positive evaluations of how well the beneficiary is accomplishing the task of providing information, among other things. More indirectly, it includes acting on the understanding of that perspective by offering advice, even when not germane to the purpose of the hearing. Once again, in the telephonic hearings, female hearing officers took the perspective of beneficiaries more commonly than did male hearing officers. In the face-to-face hearings, male hearing officers approximate the success of females, largely because physical proximity encourages social relationships such as taking the perspective of the other.

Avoiding Displays of Knowledge

It is paradoxical that a hearing officer, in whom confidence is placed to be, technically at least, a judge in a dispute, faces the need to downplay his or her own knowledge. Such downplaying seems, and is, illogical from the perspective of the traditional court setting. On the other hand, the hearing is not a traditional court setting. It is identified by virtually all hearing officers as informal (not bound by the trial register), fact-finding (not focused on persuasive rhetoric), and lacking the conventional rules of evidence (not a law case, as such). Furthermore, the hearing requires a dramatic shift of register at phase ten, one that has the broadest latitude for beneficiaries to say whatever is on their minds. Much has been said in this analysis about how crucial this phase is for accomplishing the admitted goal of bringing forth information that is explanatory of, or in addition to, the facts already represented in the record. At this point, the hearing becomes, in the most successful hearings, an informal conversation, largely because beneficiaries are more accustomed to this style and can more effectively communicate in it.

Thus, parity of status and power becomes increasingly important in phase ten. The revelation of self is encouraged by parity. If the beneficiary does not know or understand something, it can be encouraging to realize that the other person also does not know or understand something. This makes the participants equal travelers on the road to resolution. This is not to say that hearing officers should (or do) feign ignorance of what they do know. Hearings in which this strategy is evident, on the contrary, show hearing officers admitting lack of knowledge about things that do not especially impair their integrity or credentials. Their admissions are of human things, such as how to pronounce a name and difficulty with the legibility and interpretation of documents. All humans have such problems and, by admitting such vulnerability, the hearing officers are, in a sense, leveling the playing field and saying to the beneficiary, in essence, "It's okay to be vulnerable; I'm the same as you."

Direct and performative evidence of hearing officers who display their knowledge serves as a touchstone for what most hearing officers did not do. The cooperative principle of conversation specifies that participants should make their contributions as informative as required, but not to say more than is required. Only one of the telephonic hearings analyzed here gave evidence of the hearing officer displaying more knowledge and information than was required.

The in-person hearings analyzed in this study provided no examples of unnecessary displays of knowledge. The hearing officers consistently offered humanizing examples of their failure to understand (i.e., "I was wondering about one thing. The diagnosis says chronic pulmonary disease. I don't understand this. Were any other terms used?"). By explaining his own lack of understanding, this male hearing officer avoided directly challenging what might otherwise be considered conflicting information. But he was not there to win an argument, as noted earlier, by displaying his superior knowledge.

Gender Differences

In light of the professed goal of the hearing—to bring out the facts hitherto unavailable to the carrier and to explain facts that were already available—the language generally revealed by female hearing officers in telephonic hearings comes closer to achieving that goal than does the language used by male hearing officers in the telephonic hearings. This generalization holds true for all of the language features analyzed here. This is not to say that all female hearing officers were always successful with all of these language features. Nor is it to say that none of the male hearing officers were successful with any of these features. Indeed, it was pointed out above that two of the female hearing officers used what might be considered male language behavior in many of these features, and one male hearing officer used what might be considered female language behavior, at least in some instances.

Socially Acquired Gender Specification

Address Forms

There are two types of language differences related to gender: socially acquired gender specification and biologically grounded gender differences. The language features studied here are of both types.

This gender difference issue is not simply a matter to be studied and repaired, even assuming that female language behavior is preferred. Certain aspects of female language, as evidenced in this study, are simply unavailable to males. For example, certain penalties can accrue to males by addressing older people by their first names. A male addressing either male or female beneficiaries is more easily considered as too forward or condescending than is a female addressing female beneficiaries (for a female addressing male beneficiaries, however, the same penalty may accrue).

Feedback Markers

Likewise, with feedback markers, female hearing officers have the advantage of a larger inventory of possibilities socially available to them. It may sound ludicrous, for example, for a male to punctuate a beneficiary's turn of talk with a multitude of "uh-huh" feedback markers the way females are allowed to do. In addition, female intonation allowances permit "uh-huh" to be uttered with higher rising intonation, as the contrast illustrates in Figure 5-3.

Intonational gender differences are learned very early by males and females and are preserved unconsciously as a linguistic identification of gender. There is no way to change this successfully, and no particular reason to do so.

Intonation

One of the most marked gender differences in language is the use of intonation. By adolescence, males learn to reduce the range of pitch and

Figure 5-3. Intonation Contrast

stress in their voices and to produce a more monotone quality to their sentences. Although broad variation in intonation remains as available to males as it is to females, males tend to limit their use of it to information emphasis and grammatical markings, language functions where there are really no other good alternatives. Males reduce intonation variation dramatically in the emotional function (attitudinal meaning), while females make ample use of this function. The result of this gender differentiation in the use of variable intonation is that males are believed to sound more flat or monotonous than females.

The female telephonic hearing officers in this study clearly preserve this differentiation, but especially so with female beneficiaries, while male hearing officers tend to use considerably less variety in their intonation. Interestingly enough, the male hearing officers in the face-to-face hearing produce a slightly higher range of variability in intonation than male telephone counterparts, but by no means as varied as the females.

Biological Differentiation

The differences between male and female speech may also reflect biological differentiation. Females are said to be born with a disposition to establish and maintain social relationships, to hold the social group together, and to nurture. Males are said to be born with a disposition to challenge, to fight, to hunt prey, and provide for their families. It is not surprising, then, to see male hearing officers produce more direct and frightening warnings, to challenge a beneficiary's inconsistencies, to flaunt their own power through personal pronouns and, in general, to consider the hearing as a battle to be won or lost. It is equally predictable to see female hearing officers carefully knitting together a social relationship with the beneficiary, offering personal comments, sharing vulnerability, offering to let other persons tell their story, and taking their perspective when they do so.

Once again, that is not to say that the male and female hearing officers studied here fit these gender patterns completely. They do not. We have noted how certain male hearing officers accomplish what may be considered female language behavior, and how certain female officers sometimes adopt so-called male speaking patterns, even in telephonic hearings. But the generalization holds nonetheless.

Unlike the socially acquired gender differences involving address forms, feedback markers, and intonation variability, the biologically or chemically given differences can be more easily manipulated. It may seem ludicrous for a male to use the female intonation, but it is perfectly acceptable for a male to mitigate a warning or avoid a challenge. It is perfectly acceptable for a male to offer personal comments, to share power, to permit someone else to self-generate, to defuse the legal format, to take the perspective of the other person, and to avoid displaying their knowledge.

It is in these areas, in fact, that we find the male hearing officers in the face-to-face hearings using what, in the telephonic hearings, might be considered female language features. The male is no longer limited in his role to that of a fighting, hunting, dominating, all-knowing, chest-thumping, totally independent human. The testosterone is still there, however, and the possibility for slippage always present. The point here is that female hearing officers tend to be advantaged in most of the language features that make for a successful revelation of facts by beneficiaries. Males are not so naturally endowed, and they have to work to free themselves of their social and biological predispositions.

With this in mind, it is instructive to review the language behavior of the male in-person hearing officers, and to note that they were virtually as effective as the most effective female telephonic hearing officers in all of the above discussed language features except the socially acquired gender differences of variable intonation, feedback markers, and address forms. Likewise, one of the male telephonic hearing officers came close to the success of the male in-person hearing officers in many of the language features.

Physical Presence vs. Presence of Telephonic Voice Only

The opinion survey of hearing officers noted earlier pointed out certain advantages that in-person hearings were thought to have over telephonic hearings, including the following tangible features:

- conversational repair is easier to accomplish
- evidence of pain or impairment is visible
- witness demeanor and credibility can be better assessed
- communication through body language is accessible
- arguments are easier to make
- beneficiaries' language problems are easier to deal with
- reference to documents is easier
- need for adjustments to hearing problems can be more easily predicted

In various sections throughout this report, reference was made to each of these opinions, and evidence from actual hearings was cited. It is also useful, however, to focus specifically on the issue of physical presence as a discrete outcome of this analysis.

One undergirding principle of communication is that the social relationship of the participants is more collaborative and cooperative in face-to-face interaction than it is under conditions of physical separation, such as either telephonic or written communication dictate. That is, people tend to mitigate or avoid criticizing, complaining, warning, challenging, threatening, and denying when it is necessary to accomplish these speech acts face-to-face. Telephonic interaction removes some of the barriers to using such negative speech acts. Written communication removes even more barriers.

Conclusion

The findings noted above were submitted to the National Senior Citizens Law Center, which then distributed a longer version to interested parties, including the bureaucracies for which it was most appropriate. One might easily speculate on the usefulness of research such as this to the government agencies that might make use of it. At the time of this writing, I have no idea whether or not the findings represented here were useful to the bureaucracy or, in fact, whether this report was even read by them. Unlike a court case, which requires specific actions, or training, which permits the trainer to observe at least the performance and reactions of the trainees, research merely reports its findings, somewhat like tossing bread on the water and hoping that someone finds it.

Chapter 6

Facing the Bureaucratic Language of the Insurance Industry: A Case Study of a Consumers' Affairs Conference

The idea that the bureaucracies of government and industry should "do something" about the unnecessarily complex and user unfriendly language found in their efforts to communicate with the public raises its head periodically. Meetings are held, papers are written, and speeches are given. Almost everyone agrees that such language should be clearer and more accessible to the consumer and vows are made to do better. Then other priorities and crises arise and these good intentions tend to get sidetracked. Linguists have often noted that it is very hard to get language issues into the public discussion and even harder to achieve understanding of our points about language. Once in a while, however, linguists get a chance to at least join the public discussion. This chapter is about one such opportunity.

On May 15 and 16, 1978, the U.S. Office of Consumer Affairs and the National Consumers League sponsored a Washington conference on life insurance issues of concern to consumers. Representatives of business, government, the consuming public, and academia were given the opportunity to exchange views on the topics of insurance policy marketing, cost disclosure, and what this conference referred to as "policy language simplification." There were eight speakers on the topic of cost disclosure, thirteen speakers on the topic of marketing and sales practices, and four speakers on the topic of policy language simplification, including an actuary, a regulator, an insurance company representative, and a linguist.

After a welcome by the special assistant to the president for consumer affairs, Esther Peterson, an overview of the life insurance industry was presented by the acting director of the office of consumer affairs, Lee Richardson, who pointed out that a 1975 report showed that only eleven percent of policyholders bother to check their policies after purchase because "policies are too hard to read." (*New York Business*, July/August, 1975). Richardson considered this a good argument for what he referred to as "simplification." He then noted arguments in opposition to policy language simplification, which contend that as a legal contract, an insurance policy requires technical phrasing for legal precision, due to tight state regulation and precedents established in the courts. He pointed out that legislation for policy language simplification had been proposed in Congress and in state legislatures, and that such legislation had already been enacted in Vermont, New York, and Texas, while California, Pennsylvania, and Florida were beginning to move toward similar legislation.

The first panel was on the topic of policy language simplification, with a representative of an insurance company, Ron McDonald of Sentry Insurance Company; a regulator, William Woodyard, III, commissioner of insurance in Arkansas; an actuary, J. Ross Hanson, president of J. Ross Hanson, Inc.; and a linguist, Roger Shuy of Georgetown University, composing the panel. All of the speakers except the actuary, Mr. Hanson, expressed varying degrees of enthusiasm and support for the current efforts of regulators and consumer advocates to bring about insurance policy simplification.

At times Hanson outright rejected the assumption that the language of insurance policies was a problem, and at other times he supported ongoing efforts of certain insurance companies to make policies "more comprehensible," even to the extent of making use of "more descriptive policy language and the utilization of linguistic experts in drafting policies." He clearly opposed attempts to regulate in the name of policy simplification, taking the position that consumers and regulators have more important issues to deal with than language.

In order to present Hanson's stance as clearly as possible, I quote from the conference proceedings (U.S. Office of Consumer Affairs 1978) his actual presentation, as follows:

> Now, the competitive system is not perfect, and perfect equity between policyholders and shareholders is not possible. There certainly may be areas where consumers may need some assistance, such as a useful system of cost disclosure; effective control of improper sales practices, including improper advertising and

> unjustified replacements; and mutually fair claims settlement. But the language in life insurance policy forms is not one of these areas (p. 36).

Hanson then turns the problem on its head, claiming that it is the consumers who cheat the insurance companies, not the reverse:

> In the first place, as far as I know, there is very little evidence that policyholders have been cheated by the policy language. The promises made in the life insurance policy are rather simple, and even exclusions in such riders as the accidental death benefit are straightforward. In the discussions I have read, litigated claims much more often involve the policyholder trying to cheat the insurance company, by making a claim which requires a stretch of the imagination to assume it is covered under the policy. Over the years, case law has distilled the meaning of the contract which has, properly so, been construed against the insurer whenever there was ambiguity. So, in my opinion, it is simply nonsense to insist that policy language be simplified for the benefit of the consumer (p. 36).

Hanson's distinction between readability and comprehensibility is much less clear. He offers the following observations about this:

> But what about readability? This is, of course, not the same concept as comprehensibility. While a policy which is totally unreadable must therefore be incomprehensible, it does not follow that by improving readability we will necessarily improve comprehensibility. I really do not see that much benefit is gained from the use of "We/you" language. That is a purely cosmetic device. It is also easy to see that it can cause ambiguity. If some of us think that a more friendly, colloquial, less legalistic sound improves the contract, that is a matter of opinion, but it is not consumerism. Consumerism with regard to the policy is assuring that all proper claims will be paid (p. 36).

In these objections, Hanson makes it clear that he, along with most of the participants in the conference, confused the difference between simplicity and clarity. He sets up a contrast between readability and comprehensibility rather than one between simplicity and clarity. He elaborates this point in the following remarks as he attacks the Flesch readability test which, of course, is only one measure of readability, and not a very good one at that.

The Flesch test gained popularity largely because of Flesch's popular books on reading, in particular *The Art of Readable Writing* (1949).

> There seems to be a desire in some states to improve readability standards. A measure proposed by Dr. Rudolph F. Flesch, and therefore called the Flesch test, is often recommended. In essence, this test says that if the policy contains shorter sentences and, more importantly, words of few syllables, it will be more readable. That could be true, but will it benefit the consumer? I don't see how. No relationship has been established between a good Flesch score on a life insurance policy and improved comprehension (p. 37).

Hanson is, of course, quite right about the problem of relying on readability formulas to create understandable insurance policy prose. As Davison and Kantor (1982) point out, the factors measured by such formulas are not the only ones relevant to this process and do not define the actual features of texts which make them easy or hard to read. Simply shortening long, complex sentences can make the text match the readability formulas, but such changes are not always the most successful, and some may actually make the text harder to comprehend, since they can also remove the relationships between the resulting shorter sentences. Davison and Kantor cite many examples of long sentences which, when reduced to shorter ones, befog the writer's intended purpose, as the following (p. 194) will illustrate:

A. We set out basins to catch the raindrops so that we would have water to drink.

B. We had water to drink after that. We set out basins and caught the raindrops.

Example B contains two simple sentences with seven and eight words respectively, well within the limits of readability according to most readability formulas. Example A contains one complex sentence of sixteen words. But by revising sentence A to meet the formula requirements, the adaptation loses Example A's explicit causality statements ("basins to catch the raindrops" and "so that we would have water to drink"). The writer's intention is reduced to a sequence of reported facts and information. In this case, the writer's thoughts about purposeful actions are gone from the text.

Likewise, simply substituting a commonly known vocabulary concept for a more difficult one may require the use of a paraphrase, which once again makes the sentence longer. In addition, some words simply do not have easier or more frequently used synonyms. Synonymy is, in fact, something of a myth, as anyone who has ever tried to write dictionary definitions will attest. "Peace" and "tranquillity" may be considered synonyms, but they are by no means mutually substitutable for each other (as, for example, in "tranquillity conference").

Nor do readability formulas measure words or ideas that must be inferred. Information which is not explicitly expressed, or which requires inferential interpretation, may more easily lead to comprehension failure than do short sentences and words. Obviously, the need to be as explicit as possible, not causing the reader to have to infer or guess the meaning, is far more relevant to comprehensibility than sentence or word length.

So Hanson's criticism is probably right; no relationship has indeed been established between a good Flesch score on a life insurance policy and improved comprehension. But this does not mean that life insurance policies are therefore off the hook. It means only that Flesch scores have little or nothing to do with the relevant features of comprehension. They deal only with surface aspects of words and sentences.

The opening presentations of the conference made several things clear about the participants' perceptions of language issues in relation to insurance policies. It had already become obvious that the speakers viewed language as a bunch of discrete units, whether words or sentences, that they had little understanding of the difference between clarity and simplicity, and that past efforts at improving insurance policy language focused on assessing text against readability formulas that were constructed on the principle that short is better than long. This is not surprising, since these beliefs are held by many non-linguists, including many educators. It was in light of these beliefs that I grounded my presentation. The following is a modified version of my contribution to the proceedings (pp. 19–34).

When most people think of language, they think of words. It is not surprising, then, that complex language is generally thought to be the result of only complex terminology. Linguists, on the other hand, see language complexity in quite a different light. Words, the terminology, constitute the easiest part of language learning. It is much more difficult to master the structure of language, and even more difficult to learn how to use it appropriately in a multitude of contexts with a multitude of different people.

When we analyze a language for its simplicity or clarity, we see just part of the picture if we look only at words or terminology. We need to learn how that terminology fits into sentences and larger units of discourse, and we need to examine the conventional knowledge about complexity to see what interference such conventions may have on actual understanding.

Aspects of Language that Contribute to Comprehensibility

The search for textual clarity, readability, and comprehension has been evident for the past few decades. Some people assume that shorter passages and shorter words are easier to read than are longer ones. Other people look primarily at the presence or absence of jargon as a key indicator. Both groups may have the protection of the consumer in mind and both are, of course, only partly right. Linguists who have been analyzing written documents, including insurance policies, have come to the conclusion that the presence of certain terminology, though important, is not as critical to clarity as is the way such terminology is used. And here a general principle emerges. The language of insurance policies will be easily comprehensible to the extent that they (1) are predictable or naturally adhere to the patterns of ordinary discourse, and (2) allow readers to use their tacit knowledge of the conventions of their language as they try to understand it.

The demands of an insurance policy seem to be three:

1. That it be explicitly informative
2. That it be technically accurate
3. That it be legally true

The language of insurance policies is different from oral language because it has to convey its meaning effectively on any occasion over an extended period of time. The problem of how to do this is a very serious linguistic one.

One exciting thing about language is that it provides alternative ways of expressing a given meaning. But each alternative structure functions differently, and a different context may offer still further shades of possible meaning. Since linguists study ambiguity, there is already a large body of knowledge available about how such ambiguity occurs. For example, some writing experts have begun to recommend that passive constructions be avoided in favor of active verbs. Although the passive is often overused or ineffectively used in documents such as insurance policies, there are times when the passive can be more effective and, in at least one sense of the term, can actually be clearer than the active voice. Note the substitution of active for passive in the following sentences taken from an insurance policy:

passive: 44 CFR Chapter 5 is vacated and reserved.

active: We vacate and reserve 44 CFR Chapter 5.

Not only does the active version reorder the emphasis of the sentence, making the relevant CFR unit less prominent, but it also specifies a totally irrelevant subject and, in linguistic terms, overloads the complement of the verb. In this case, the active voice may not be as clear and effective as the passive.

But the point here is not that the active or passive is generally better or worse. It is that there are contexts in which one or the other is more appropriate, and in which choosing one or the other conveys a different meaning than in other contexts. Simple global statements about avoiding the passive cannot be made, and the consumer will not necessarily be protected by such statements. The sheer size of one of the noun phrases makes the active voice, in version (1) of the following regulatory text, much harder to understand than the corresponding passive voice in version (2):

1. (active voice version)

> The purpose of this Regulation is to protect the purchaser from misrepresentation, unfair comparisons and deceptive and misleading sales methods in the solicitation of a life insurance contract. Requiring disclosure of certain information pertinent to the life insurance contract, and further prohibiting certain acts or practices which are deceptive, misleading, or which misrepresent the terms of a life insurance policy or life insurance benefit, or in some way are contrary to Pennsylvania statutes, can best achieve this purpose.

2. (passive voice version)

> The purpose of this Regulation is to protect the purchaser from misrepresentation, unfair comparisons, and deceptive and misleading sales methods in the solicitation of a life insurance contract. This purpose can best be achieved by requiring disclosure of certain information pertinent to the life insurance contract, and by further prohibiting certain acts or practices which are deceptive, misleading, or which misrepresent the terms of a life insurance policy or life insurance benefit, or in some way are contrary to Pennsylvania statutes.

A skeletal reconstruction of the two sentences of each version yields the following:

(1) active voice version

Sentence 1 Purpose of the Regulation.

Sentence 2 Requiring . . . (5 lines of things) . . . can best achieve this purpose.

(2) passive voice version

Sentence 1 Purpose of the Regulation.
Sentence 2 This purpose can be achieved by . . . (5 lines of things).

It is clear that adopting the active voice here causes the main verb to be delayed for some five lines of text, a strain on any reader's ability to endure. In this case, using the active voice also removes the cohesive tie that connects the first sentence with the second, in this case the use of the sentence connector, "this," accompanied by the repetition of the main point of the first sentence, "purpose." If the adapter were to simply apply the principle that active voice verbs should always replace the passive, comprehensibility could suffer from the very effort made to enhance it. The bad news may be that linguistic analysis usually reveals the complications of such simplistic rules of thumb, such as, "always avoid the passive voice," but the good news is that linguistic analysis also explains where and why these simplistic rules fail and, at the same time, offers ways to solve the problem. Important decisions are made possible by accurately identifying the topic of the text and then by determining what information should be emphasized, as opposed to what information is less relevant to the point being made.

Another area of potential language complexity includes the use of nominal versus verbal expressions. Insurance policies seem to have a strong preference for nominal forms, such as the following:

The death of the insured	vs.	when the insured dies
Make an election	vs.	elect (or choose)

Such nominal constructions tend to suppress the agent of the action and they can lead to comprehension difficulties for the consumer, since language research has shown that nominals are more difficult for readers to process. But again, we cannot make a simple blanket rule against the use of nominals because such expressions have very legitimate roles to play in writing. One of these roles is to soften the potentially harsh impact of certain possible eventualities, such as death or other tragedies. Suppose, for example, the airline attendant's safety instruction announcement, "in case of a water landing," were revised to "in case we crash into the ocean." The nominal form is clearly less frightening and probably to be preferred. Whether or not the consumer is better protected by "water landing" is open to question, but the fact is that we can set no universal rule for verbals over nominals.

The linguistic analysis of text also deals with clause embedding, conditionals, ellipsis, and anaphora. These are terms that linguists use to represent phenomena that others may know by other names. Anaphora, for example, describes references which are substituted for or omitted in an expression, such as pronouns for nouns, with much the same force and designation. Likewise, verbs can be omitted in sentences such as "Fred ate spinach and Melvin broccoli," where "ate" is assumed to be broccoli's verb. In an effort to be explicit, insurance policies sometimes repeat the same noun phrase over and over, avoiding all anaphoric referencing. This is thought to reduce vagueness, but it can also be quite unpredictable. Being clear at the level of vocabulary does not ensure that clarity is maintained at the discourse level of language. Consumers are used to reading and hearing prose that follows normal, predictable discourse rules. The following paragraph, taken from a policy, has explicit referencing at the word level but, at the discourse level, has an odd and unpredictable ring. In an effort to make co-reference relations between noun phrases perfectly explicit, documents sometimes forego the use of pronouns altogether. This results in language that is quite different from spoken language or other forms of written language, as the following example shows:

> In the event that **Tenant** shall have ceased to occupy the dwelling unit, and shall have removed substantially all of **Tenant's** furniture therefrom without having given the aforesaid notice of an anticipated extended absence, then Landlord at such time shall have the right to treat the dwelling unit as having been abandoned by **Tenant**.

First, readers are asked to process a fifty-four word sentence, with three dependent clauses preceding the main clause (beginning at the thirty-fifth word). They must also translate legal (or pseudo-legal) phrasings such as "ceased to occupy," "aforesaid," and the bothersome, unlifelike use of "shall," where "will" or, in one case, the present progressive "has," are more natural and predictable. They must also understand that "Tenant" and "Landlord" are legal objects of some type that, for some reason, no longer need to be prefaced by "the." Then, on top of this, the writer decides to abandon pronoun references (see the bolded repetitions of Tenant).

If one were to suggest that the above list contains problems suitable for revision, critics such as Mr. Hanson reply that these suggestions are "purely cosmetic." He complained, in fact, that "a more friendly, colloquial, less legalistic" language is not consumerism. He, along with others, seems to conceive of "friendly" prose as colloquial rather than predictable. Perhaps insurance specialists simply do not see that non-specialists do not share their own language practices, knowledge, and schemas. Perhaps this helps to explain why patients are often confused by their doctors' advice or why witnesses in court are sometimes confused by the law-friendly but not lay-friendly questions of lawyers. Perhaps asking the insurance industry to identify the language that unacculturated consumers might not understand is asking too much. Perhaps the fox should not be expected to guard the henhouse.

In any case, when we recently examined a number of insurance policies, we also noted the tendency to repeat other words over and over, as follows:

> Paid-up Dividend Additions. Used as a net single premium at the attained age of the Insured to purchase additional paid-up life insurance, called "paid-up dividend additions," which will also participate in dividends and will have increasing cash and loan values. The cash value of paid-up dividend additions will equal the net single premium for the additions at the attained age of the Insured on the date the value is determined. Any paid-up dividend additions in force at the death of the Insured will be added to the policy proceeds.

Assuming that the readers know the meaning of "additions," "dividends," "participate," and "attained age" here, and assuming that they can get over the lack of grammatical subject in the first sentence, they are still faced with the unfamiliarity of the repeated underlined words (these were underlined in the policy). One might argue that such repetition is used to teach the policy holder the special language of insurance, leaving open the question about whether or not such teaching is necessary or appropriate. If this justification is examined carefully, however, one could counter that there are ways of doing this teaching that conform to the way we often teach people new terms and concepts: by appositional definitions. One might have said, for example, "paid-up dividend additions, by which we mean . . . ," or "cash value, that is . . . " This is how good teachers do this.

There was a time when teaching children how to read stressed what was called "repeated reinforcement." Beginning reading materials were replete with examples such as the following:

> Jill said, "Help Ben, Bill.
> Stop the ducks.
> Help Ben stop the ducks."

Here Jill's third sentence does not add anything new to the discourse. It merely repeats the content of the first two. The theory of repeated reinforcement, however good it was, clashed uncomfortably with another theory—that readers build on what they already know in order to learn what they do not already know, predicting the unknown from the known. As it turns out, this theory is also an important theory of discourse, called the given-new principle. Any repetition that yields unpredictable text blocks readers from calling on what they know about how language works or how the real world works as they try to learn what they do not know.

We may laugh at the inordinate repetition of basal reader texts, such as the following, but the decision to use repetition to avoid possible confusion can be equally humorous.

> Jill said, "What do turtles like to do?"
> Nan said, "Turtles like to hide."
> "Turtles like to eat."
> "But what will this turtle eat?"
> Bill said, "Turtles like to swim."
> "But this turtle can't swim here."

The repetition of "turtles" in every sentence marks this passage as reading text prose. It also gives the impression that the reader is a novice, and it may even sound a bit condescending. Such repetition runs counter to natural principles of discourse organization. Pronominal forms and other substitute nominals enable us to avoid continuously repeated noun phrases such as this. The above discourse would sound much more natural if "they" were at least sometimes used in place of "turtles," and "this one" for "this turtle." The use of pronouns also indicates that there is a connection between what we are talking about in one sentence and what we are talking about in another, adding cohesion to the overall text. Consumers, who have to rely on their tacit knowledge of how language works, will not be well served by such efforts at achieving clarity.

To understand an insurance policy, a consumer must also infer a great deal. Again, the subject of inference is a linguistic topic since inferencing is guided by the structure of the text. How sentences are connected provides one the major task of inferencing. A text that is composed of short, independent sentences places a greater demand on the reader to infer the relationships between sentences than does a text with longer sentences with such relationships built in. For example, one paragraph in an insurance policy was transformed from long sentences to short ones, resulting in the following:

> A premium might remain in default after the end of its grace period. Any cash surrender value of the Policy will be used. The Policy will be continued in force. It will be paid-up insurance or extended term insurance. It will be in a certain amount. The amount is determined below. No further premiums will be due.

> Any Riders will terminate. This excepts other provisions to the Rider.

Here the syntactic simplicity results in a loss of explicitness (since the sentence connections are now gone), resulting in a passage that is less easy to follow and to understand.

A major category of inferences which deserves attention concerns how the sentences in a text are understood to be connected. A text is not simply a list of independently understood sentences. Meaning, whether at the sentence or discourse level, relies on implicit connections among sentences even though many connections are never made completely explicit. Consider the following passage, for example:

> If a premium remains in default after the end of its grace period, any cash surrender value of the Policy will be used to continue the Policy in force as paid-up insurance or as extended term insurance, in an amount as determined below, and no further premiums will be due. Any Riders will terminate, unless otherwise provided to the Rider.

The second sentence cannot be understood independently from the first. The condition specified in the first sentence ("If a premium remains in default after the end of its grace period"), is equally applicable to the second sentence. Any effort to produce clearly written insurance policies will need to take into consideration how sentences cooperate with each other, explicitly or inferentially, to convey the intended meaning of the writer.

Misconceptions about Language that Interfere with Comprehensibility

Our survey of a sample of current insurance policies reveals a number of misconceptions about language which can interfere with the production of clear, comprehensible text. One way to think about such things is to consider the values and beliefs of the people whose task is to address insurance policy language.

Although it is not clear from the writing of the policies themselves, the very fact that a conference has been called to address the issue suggests strongly that clear writing is valued. Nor can there be any question about this from the words and actions of the participants. Good writing is valued, however it is defined or practiced.

It is in the area of beliefs about language that there seems to be a deep difference between the linguist and the other participants. This is not a surprise to linguists, who discover daily that non-linguists hold language beliefs that are, to us, unusual. Some of these beliefs have been mentioned already, but it may be useful to reiterate them here.

1. Language simplicity means the same thing as language clarity.

The participants, along with the documents they spoke from and cited, speak only about "simplicity" as the goal. There was an amazing absence of the use of the word, "clear." Although the speakers never explicitly stated that these two concepts are one and the same, their sole focus on "simple" suggests this belief. To understand the relationship between simplicity and clarity, we need to talk about the various aspects of how a language is put together or structured, and we need to examine the various processes that are involved in a reader's making sense out of a written text.

Consider, for example, what it might mean for a stretch of writing or speaking to be "simple." Simplicity in syntax may be accompanied by complex vocabulary. Simple vocabulary may be presented in complex syntax. Simple syntax and vocabulary may be couched in very complex discourse structure. Simplicity, therefore, cannot be defined or measured in isolation from various types or levels of language structure. Whatever comprehension danger there is for consumers can be easily overlooked if we look only at one level of language as the culprit.

2. A limited inventory of words or sentence patterns will yield clarity.

This belief or misconception about clarity may be a carry-over from the field of education, where considerable attention is given to "limited vocabulary," "controlled" spelling patterns, and the repetition of a limited number of syntactic constructions for early learners. This belief is misguided on several counts. For one thing, there have never been any acceptable studies to show exactly what the given vocabulary or syntax should be for the developmental stages of learning. Oddly enough, teaching programs that produce materials that are geared to specific "grade or age levels" are based on books and materials written by adults for children, and not by children themselves. Nor is it understood that we often introduce complexities at one level, such as syntax, as we attempt to create simplicity at another, such as vocabulary.

Alternatively, this belief may stem from the blindness of the industry to the fact that not everyone knows the same terms and concepts that insurance people know. Lawyers, doctors, and other specialists may well share such blindness about their own fields. Jargon and terms of art are perfectly appropriate when used within the specialist's group. But when used with outsiders, they can be unclear, if not off-putting.

Whatever the cause of this belief, reading insurance policies leads one to the conclusion that there has often been a concerted effort to limit the number of words used to refer to a given concept. The best interpretation one can make of this is that the writers feel that if they were to use two or three more terms for the same concept, even as appositional definitions, there would be a greater possibility of misunderstanding. The worst interpretation is that the writers are deliberately trying to keep the reader from comprehending the meaning of what is being said. Somewhere in between these extremes is the interpretation that the writers are so afraid of a lawsuit that they feel constrained to use legal language to readers who do not understand it.

Whichever motivation is accurate, the belief leads to paragraphs such as the following:

> Written notice and proof of claim must be furnished to the Home Office while the Insured is living and remains totally disabled. In event of default in payment premiums, such notice and proof of claim must also be furnished within 12 months from the due date of the premium in default. Failure to furnish notice and proof as required above shall not of itself invalidate or diminish any claim hereunder if it is shown not to have been reasonably possible to have furnished such notice and proof and that such notice and proof were furnished as soon as was reasonably possible.

It appears, for example, that the writer here assumes that substituting another term for the preferred term, "furnish," such as "supply," "submit," "provide," "give," or some other word, would result in potential misreading of the intended concept.

3. Repetition contributes to clarity.

As noted earlier, this may be true at one level, such as vocabulary, but it may at the same time confuse at the discourse level.

4. To be clear, one must be explicit.

In the case of insurance policy language, a problem seems to arise not only from the effort to be absolutely and totally explicit, but also from the desire to be absolutely and totally explicit in each sentence. For perfectly understandable reasons, insurance policies must be as accurate and explicit as possible. This goal can lead writers to think of all the real and potential conditions which might apply to any given statement. Linguistically, the result of such explicitness is a piling up of short phrases in sentences such as the following:

> The cash value of the Policy at any time while the Policy is in force on a premium-paying basis equals its cash value at the end of the period for which pre-minimums are due and paid.
>
> Unless otherwise elected in writing, if any premium remains unpaid at the end of its grace period, a premium will be paid automatically by the Company to the next quarterly premium date (a) using any available dividend accumulations and (b) advancing any available loan value of the Policy as an automatic policy loan as of the date of the unpaid premium.

This piling up can be visualized by writing the short phrases on separate lines, as follows:

> The cash value
> of the Policy
> at any time
> while the Policy is
> in force
> on a premium-paying basis
> equals its cash value
> at the end
> of the period
> for which premiums are due and paid.
> Unless otherwise elected
> in writing,
> if any premium remains unpaid
> at the end
> of its grace period,
> a premium will be paid automatically
> by the Company
> to the next quarterly premium date
> (a) using any available dividend accumulations and

(b) advancing any available loan value
of the Policy
as an automatic policy loan
as of the date
of the unpaid premium.

5. Short items are better than long ones.

This is not necessarily true, as noted above.

Conclusion

Clarity in the writing of insurance policies will provide consumer protection but the issue itself is very complex. Looking at terminology alone is only a very small part of the picture of language clarity and consumer understanding.

It should not be surprising to learn that not a great deal is known about how the aspects of language contribute to clarity and how they interfere in the specific context of insurance policies. Linguists have made an important first step but a great deal remains to be done. Far too often, complex issues are seen as simple ones, and when treatment that is based on superficial knowledge fails, the issue is unresolved. Even good ideas, when superficially treated, lose credibility. The history of American education's continual efforts to find simple answers to complex problems is a sobering example.

The search for finding ways to protect the consumer of insurance policies through clearly written and comprehensible prose might benefit from the parallels with children's language learning. When children learn their native language they learn more than words and surface sentence patterns in which to fit the words. They also learn a system that allows them to put meaning in appropriate and acceptable forms. They learn a system that enables them to link one form to another and one sentence to another, in order to form a coherent and understandable whole. Learning to write clear insurance policies is not all that different.

There is a certain amount of verbal art to the way we apply the language system that we learned as children. Some people learn to write and speak more ably than others. But we each have the system as part of our linguistic competence. It is what enables us to communicate with each other and understand what others say and write.

The first recommendation that linguists might make for achieving greater clarity in the prose of insurance policies is to make that prose more consonant with the consumer's already existing linguistic system. Both the positive and the negative examples discussed above involve the readers' ability to use their natural linguistic system when they read an insurance policy. Some attempts to make insurance prose clear and precise superimpose considerations that contradict the readers' natural language competence. We have yet to make the best use of what we already know about this issue, and there is a great deal more still to be learned. Linguists stand ready to help.

Chapter 7

Untangling the Bureaucratic Language of Real Estate: A Case Study of Commission Agreements

It is probably obvious that the real estate business has its own special bureaucracy. I occasionally get a glimpse of it in my work with the various types of agreements and contracts used in that industry. It seems that whether the topic is Medicare, the reports of physicians, insurance policies, or, as in this case, written agreements about the commissions accruing to real estate agents, the language structure of a bureaucracy is present. Of the definitions of "bureaucracy" mentioned in the foreword to this book, the meaning which referred to "excessive red tape and routine" seems most relevant here. Language, of course, is not immune to routines which often become difficult to understand or ambiguous.

Real estate transactions are carried out by real estate agents, brokers, or salespersons. For their efforts, they are entitled to payment for their services in the form of commissions, usually calculated as a percentage of the total paid for the transaction. A commission agreement is prepared in advance of the transaction, stating as clearly as possible exactly how this calculation is based. Once the transaction has been agreed to by the owner and the lessor or purchaser, agents can demand their commissions as set forth in that commission agreement.

As simple as this process may seem, complications can arise when there is more than one property involved in the agreement, when there is more than one commission agreement in effect, when the commission agreement includes, or can be interpreted to include, not only sales, but also leases, and when the exact description of the property or properties is interpreted in more than one way. All of these complications are associated with the case described here.[1]

Background

In the mid-seventies, a real estate agent named Roy Green[2] entered into an agreement with Aldena Coastal Properties, Inc. to be the agent for transactions involving various properties owned by that company. The agreement, in fact, was embodied in three different commission agreements in an eleven-months period. The first agreement, related to a lease, is dated October 31, 1975. The second was related to a supplemental lease, called Supplemental Lease Agreement No. 1, dated March 8, 1976. The third commission agreement was related to another lease agreement, No. GS-04B-15540, dated October 6, 1976.

By the time I became involved in this matter, both agent Green and the property owner had come to a standstill about how to resolve their conflict about the commission agreements. Both sides had hired attorneys and the matter was headed for court. I was called by the attorneys for Aldena Coastal Properties, Inc., to determine whether or not their position in this case was the proper and accurate interpretation of the commission agreements. In keeping with my practice of trying to maintain as much neutrality as possible, I was not told what their position was, but it was not very difficult to figure out in this case. Clearly, the broker believed that he was entitled to commissions that the owner did not believe were justified by their commission agreements. Nor was I told what other evidence their side might have, if any, in the matter. All I received from Aldena's attorneys were the commission agreements themselves.

In contrast with other cases described in this book, the issue put before me was not how to improve the written language to make it more comprehensible or to make global suggestions to the entire industry, as in the case of the insurance bureaucracy portrayed in Chapter 6. My task in this case was much more focused. It dealt only with the referencing found in the commission agreements in evidence in this case. I was to try to make sense out of an almost hopelessly garbled anaphoric practice and to determine, if possible, what referred to what. In places where the referencing could

[1] All references to specific people, organizations, and places have been changed to protect the anonymity of the participants.
[2] This chapter is based in part on my earlier analysis in Steele and Threadgold (eds.) 1987.

not be clearly identified, I was to point out the range of possible references based on linguistic knowledge. And I was to do all this in ways that could be understood by the court. Toward this end, I prepared an affidavit containing the following information.

As any linguist knows full well, things that are clear enough to us have a way of being unclear to people outside our field. I have learned that it is useful to try to develop a visual method of explaining language matters. Some twenty years' experience as an expert witness have taught me that some people respond to pictures, some to numbers, and some to words. But even the word people, when faced with linguistic issues, often retreat to stony silence or indifference. One cursory reading of the materials sent me for analysis made it very clear that anaphora was the battleground here. After some experimenting with various ways to illustrate this issue, I hit upon the metaphor of a chain, which led me to try to describe anaphoric referencing as a chaining event, with each new defined reference changing and controlling the anaphoric links that followed.

Commission Agreement Number One

The chaining began as follows. The preamble to the first commission agreement defines the property in question as that which is referenced by Exhibit A, "together with the entire water frontage bordering the property described herein." Following the rules of English language referencing, subsequent references to "property" or "said property" are understood to refer to that property, both as it is described in Exhibit A and in the addendum words "together with." As is the custom in English, any new meanings intended by the writers or signers of this agreement must be newly designated. Anaphora works as a chaining sequence as follows: Defined Reference > Anaphoric Reference 1 > Anaphoric Reference 2, and so on. If an intervening reference is introduced or if the writer's intention is to alter the meaning of the defined reference, such activity must be marked by a new definition. Otherwise, it is the accepted convention of English to understand that anaphoric references are to the original defined reference.

I noted that paragraph eight of Commission Agreement No. 1 clearly illustrates a change in the marked or defined reference to property. With specific reference to the name, Waterford Plaza, at 643 Denmark Avenue, this paragraph marks a new property reference chain. This was necessary since the burden of this paragraph is to exclude Waterford Plaza as commissionable to Mr. Green. Thus the chaining sequence has been broken as shown in Figure 7-1.

Property	
Defined Reference No. 1	(in preamble) Exhibit A, together with the entire water frontage bordering the property described
Anaphoric Reference	(in preamble) The property
Anaphoric Reference	(in preamble) said property
Defined Reference No. 2	(in paragraph 8) Waterford Plaza, 643 Denmark Ave.
Anaphoric Reference	(in paragraph 8) said Waterford Plaza

FIGURE 7-1. **Property References (Agreement One)**

In that the conventions of English language anaphora specify that a referencing chain is broken by the introduction of a new defined reference, all references to property in paragraph eight refer to Waterford Plaza and to no other property. This means that the words in that paragraph, "in the event any further or future lease or leases are entered into between OWNER-LESSOR and lessee," refer only to the property designated as Waterford Plaza. The meaning of this paragraph, as revealed by the referencing chain, is that this building is excepted from commission to the broker unless a separate written instrument is executed. In terms of this dispute, this paragraph excludes Mr. Green from getting a commission for being the agent who arranges the lease of this property.

In addition to anaphoric referencing related to property, these documents contain what can be called anaphora within anaphora. That is, within the unbroken anaphoric chaining sequences, subreferences exist. Because of the relationship between property and leases, references to "lease" or "leases" within a chaining sequence can be clearly identified by that chaining sequence. Thus the defined reference to "a Lease" dated the second day of October 1975 is followed by anaphoric references to that lease, as shown in Figure 7-2.

This chaining sequence indicates clearly that all references to "Lease" re-

Lease	
Defined Reference	(in preamble) a Lease dated the 2nd day of October 1975
Anaphoric Reference	(in preamble) a Lease
Anaphoric Reference	(in preamble) the Lease
Anaphoric Reference	(in paragraph 2) the Lease
Anaphoric Reference	(in paragraph 3) the basic Lease
Anaphoric Reference	(in paragraph 4) said basic or orginal Lease or based upon the present Lease
Anaphoric Reference	(in paragraph 4) said Lease
Anaphoric Reference	(in paragraph 4B) said Lease
Anaphoric Reference	(in paragraph 4C) the Lease
Anaphoric Reference	(in paragraph 4E) the Lease
Anaphoric Reference	(in paragraph 4E) the said Lease
Anaphoric Reference	(in paragraph 4E) the Lease described above
New Defined Reference	(in paragraph 8) any further or future lease or leases

FIGURE 7-2. **Lease Reference (Agreement One)**

fer to the first defined reference, a Lease dated the second day of October 1975, except for the last reference in paragraph eight, which breaks the chain by defining a new lease referent. Evidence of this can be found not only in the anaphoric chain but also in the structure of the lexicon and the capitalization practice. In the English language, a lease can be used as a first reference while the lease refers to one that is preceding. For example, we can say: "A man came today. The man fixed the stove." It is unconventional, if not confusing, to say, "The man came today. A man fixed the stove." The use of the article, "the," assumes clear referencing. The use of the article, "a," is either introductory or is not clear. Note also that all references to the specific October 2 lease begin with capital letters. This is not the case for the new defined reference, in which "lease" is in lower case.

The significance of this anaphoric referencing to property and to lease for property is as follows. It shows clearly that in Commission Agreement No. 1, all references to property up to paragraph eight are to the property defined in Exhibit A, "together with the entire water frontage bordering the property described herein," and all references to the leases up to paragraph eight are to leases related to that property only. It also shows clearly that in paragraph eight, a newly defined property reference is Waterford Plaza, and all references to leases in paragraph eight are to further or future lease or leases relating to that property only.

Commission Agreement Number Two

Commission Agreement No. 2, dated March 2, 1976, also begins with a clearly defined reference to the property under discussion as specified in Exhibit A, "together with the entire water frontage bordering the property described herein." The reference chaining system is shown in Figure 7-3.

Paragraph nine in Commission Agreement No. 2, like paragraph eight of Commission Agreement No. 1, specifies a change in the defined reference to property, marking a new property reference chain. This marking exempts Mr. Green from commission for procuring any tenant for that property "not related to the U.S. Customs Service in that specified property."

In addition to anaphoric referencing related to property, this document also contains anaphora within anaphora. Again, all references to "lease" or "leases" can be clearly identified within the property references chaining as shown in Figure 7-4.

This chaining sequence is essentially the same as the one indicated in Commission Agreement No. 1, with minor exceptions. In Commission Agreement No. 2, since this agreement must encompass a supplementary lease as well as the original lease, referencing to "lease" or "leases" is differentiated. Nevertheless, all references to the first defined reference leases are to the property defined in Exhibit A, "with the entire water frontage bordering the property described herein." The reference to "the Leases" (plural form), first in the preamble and then repeated in paragraph 2, 4E, and 5 (twice), evidences recognition of the fact that, contrary to Commission Agreement No. 1, this second agreement must take into account the original lease and the supplementary lease. Both "Lease" and "Leases," however, fall within the anaphoric chaining sequence which

Property	
Defined Reference	(in preamble) EXHIBIT A, together with the entire water frontage bordering the property described
Anaphoric Reference	(in preamble) the property
Anaphoric Reference	(in preamble) the said property
Anaphoric Reference	(in paragraph 3) the land specified
Anaphoric Reference	(in paragraph 4) the within premises
New Defined Reference	(in paragraph 9) the existing Waterford Plaza Building, at 643 Denmark Avenue
Anaphoric Reference	(in paragraph 9) said existing Waterford Plaza Building

FIGURE 7-3. **Property References (Agreement Two)**

relates to the property described clearly as defined by Exhibit A, "with the entire water frontage bordering the property described herein."

Having tried to show how anaphoric referencing works like a chain for both "property" and "leases," it now became evident that these two chains had to be put together, for together is how they appear in the commission agreements. In analyzing data, one can dissect and isolate in order to see clearly (much as a microscope dissects and isolates phenomena under inspection), but eventually the whole thing has to be reassembled to approximate its original state. Having described visually how the commission agreements' referencing worked individually for "property" and for "leases," it now behooved me to show how they worked together. Figure 7-5 represents this effort.

This visualization of the referencing sequence makes clear the anaphora to "lease(s)" in Commission Agreement No. 2. In the preamble, clear reference is first given to both Lease No. 1 and the Supplementary Lease. Next, from the preamble through paragraph two, all anaphoric references are to both of these leases (plural). Then, in paragraph three, the referencing picks up the supplementary lease again. Since it is necessary, if not obligatory for the sake of clarity, to specifically reidentify the anaphoric reference once it has been diverted (in this case by first identifying both leases individually and then by referring to them together in the plural), it is then necessary to reestablish here their individual identity if individual

Lease(s)		
Defined Reference	(in preamble) a Lease known as Supplemental Lease Agreement No. 1 to Lease #68-040-1531	
Anaphoric Reference	a Supplemental Lease	(preamble)
	The Leases	(preamble)
	as well as potential future lease additions, modifications and extension thereof	(preamble)
	The Leases	(para. 2)
	the basic Supplemental Lease	(para. 3)
	a Ten (10) year Supplemental Lease	(para. 3)
	the . . . Lease attached as Exhibit "B"	(para. 3)
	the Supplemental Lease	(para. 4)
	said Supplemental Lease	(para. 4)
	said Lease	(para. 4)
	the Lease hereinbefore referred to	(para. 4)
	this Supplemental Lease	(para. 4)
	this Supplemental Lease	(para. 4)
	The Lease Agreement	(para. 4)
	said Supplemental Lease	(para. 4B)
	the Supplemental Lease	(para. 4C)
	the Lease	(para. 4E)
	the Lease	(para. 4E)
	the Lease	(para. 4E)
	Leases in the future	(para. 4E)
	the Leases	(para. 5)
	the Leases herein referred to	(para. 5)
	the Lease	(para. 5)
New Defined Reference	(in paragraph 9) any further or future Lease or Leases not related to U.S. Customs Services	

FIGURE 7-4. Lease References (Agreement Two)

identity is to be referenced. Thus in paragraph three, this document clearly specifies that it now references the Supplemental Lease by referring to it as the "basic Supplemental Lease," "the Supplemental Lease," and "the Lease attached as Exhibit B." The thirteen following references carefully and clearly reference only the Supplemental Lease either by specific reference to "Supplemental Lease" or by chained anaphora ("said Lease" or "the Lease") which, by the rules of English anaphora, clearly specify the Supplemental Lease. Finally, from paragraph 4E to the end of this docu-

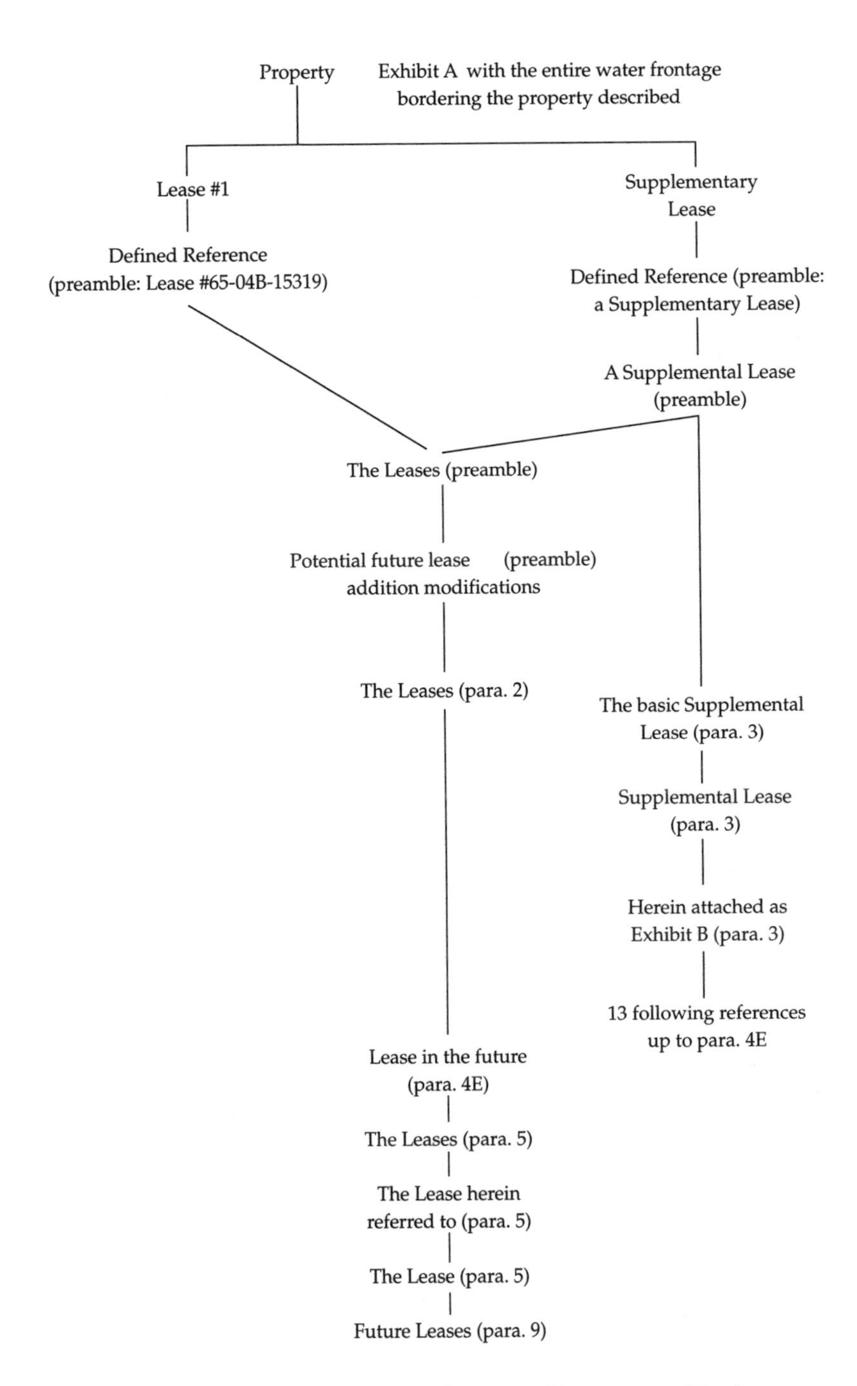

FIGURE 7-5. Property and Lease References (Agreement Two)

ment, all references to "Lease" are plural, referencing clearly the combination of both Lease No. 1 and the Supplemental Lease.

The significance of this anaphoric referencing to "property" and "lease for property" in the second document is as follows. It shows clearly that in Commission Agreement No. 2, all references to "property" up to paragraph nine are to the property defined as Exhibit A, "together with the entire water frontage bordering the property described herein" and that all references to "lease" or "leases" up to paragraph nine relate only to that property. It also shows clearly that in paragraph nine, a newly defined property reference is the existing Waterford Plaza Building, and that all references to further or future lease(s) to that property, not related to the U.S. Customs Service, are not commissionable to Mr. Green unless a separate written instrument is executed toward that end.

It should be further mentioned here that there is, in Commission Agreement No. 2, one other reference to future leases (in paragraph 4E). It is clear from the anaphoric reference in this document that this reference to "Leases in the future" is governed by the property reference to which it relates, in this case only to that which is described in Exhibit A, "together with the entire water frontage bordering the property described herein," and not to any other property.

Commission Agreement Number Three

The anaphoric referencing sequence in Commission Agreement No. 3, signed August 31, 1976, is in many ways similar to the previous two agreements. Again, in order to understand the referencing in this document, it is first necessary to clearly determine the property references.

This agreement also begins with a clearly defined reference to the property under discussion as specified in Exhibit A, further identified as 68 N.W. 22nd Avenue as shown in figure 7-6.

Paragraph ten in Commission Agreement No. 3, like paragraph eight of Commission Agreement No. 1 and paragraph nine of Commission Agreement No. 2, specifies a change in the defined referent to property, marking a new property reference chain. Again, this marking exempts Mr. Green from commission for procuring any tenant for that property that was not related to the U.S. Customs Service.

In addition to anaphoric referencing related to property, this document also contains anaphora within anaphora. Again, the reference to "lease" or "leases" can be identified clearly inside the property reference chaining. The reference chaining is different from that of the preceding commission agreements in that anaphoric references are made to two separate leases

Property	
Defined Reference	(in preamble) Exhibit A, 68 N.W. 22nd Avenue
Anaphoric Reference	(in preamble) the property
Anaphoric Reference	(in preamble) real property
Anaphoric Reference	(in paragraph 6) the property
Anaphoric Reference	(in paragraph 6) the property
New Defined Reference	(in paragraph 10) the existing Waterford Plaza Building
Anaphoric Reference	(in paragraph 10) said existing Waterford Plaza Building

FIGURE 7-6. **Property References (Agreement Three)**

individually and, on four occasions, to both leases together. This caused both parties in the case much confusion and, even though the chaining chart, Figure 7-7, may seem complex, it was ultimately deemed clearer than the prose in the written documents.

After the first combined reference to both Lease No. 1 and Lease No. 2 (in paragraph two), both defined references for these two leases are clearly reestablished by specific language (in paragraph three). The words which reestablish the topics as Lease No. 1 are "the basic Lease." When the reference shifts to Lease No. 2, the words specifically reestablish this by reading, "the aforementioned Lease No. GS-04B-15540.

The combined reference to both leases (in paragraph five G) is less specific but is clearly marked by the plural form, "Leases." When the topic shifts back to Lease No. 2 alone, the language is specific, "the Lease above described" (paragraph 5G). The language then switches to both leases almost immediately, using the plural form "Leases" once more. Then it switches back to Lease No. 2 again, with the singular form, "Lease." The last switch to the combined leases is in paragraph six, "the Leases," with an immediate return to Lease No. 2 ("the Lease") in the same paragraph.

Later in Commission Agreement No. 3, a third defined reference is introduced in paragraph ten, "further or future Lease or Leases not related to the U.S. Customs Service." This defined reference has no subsequent anaphoric references but must be set off as a separate defined reference since it refers to a new and specific property (643 Denmark Avenue) from

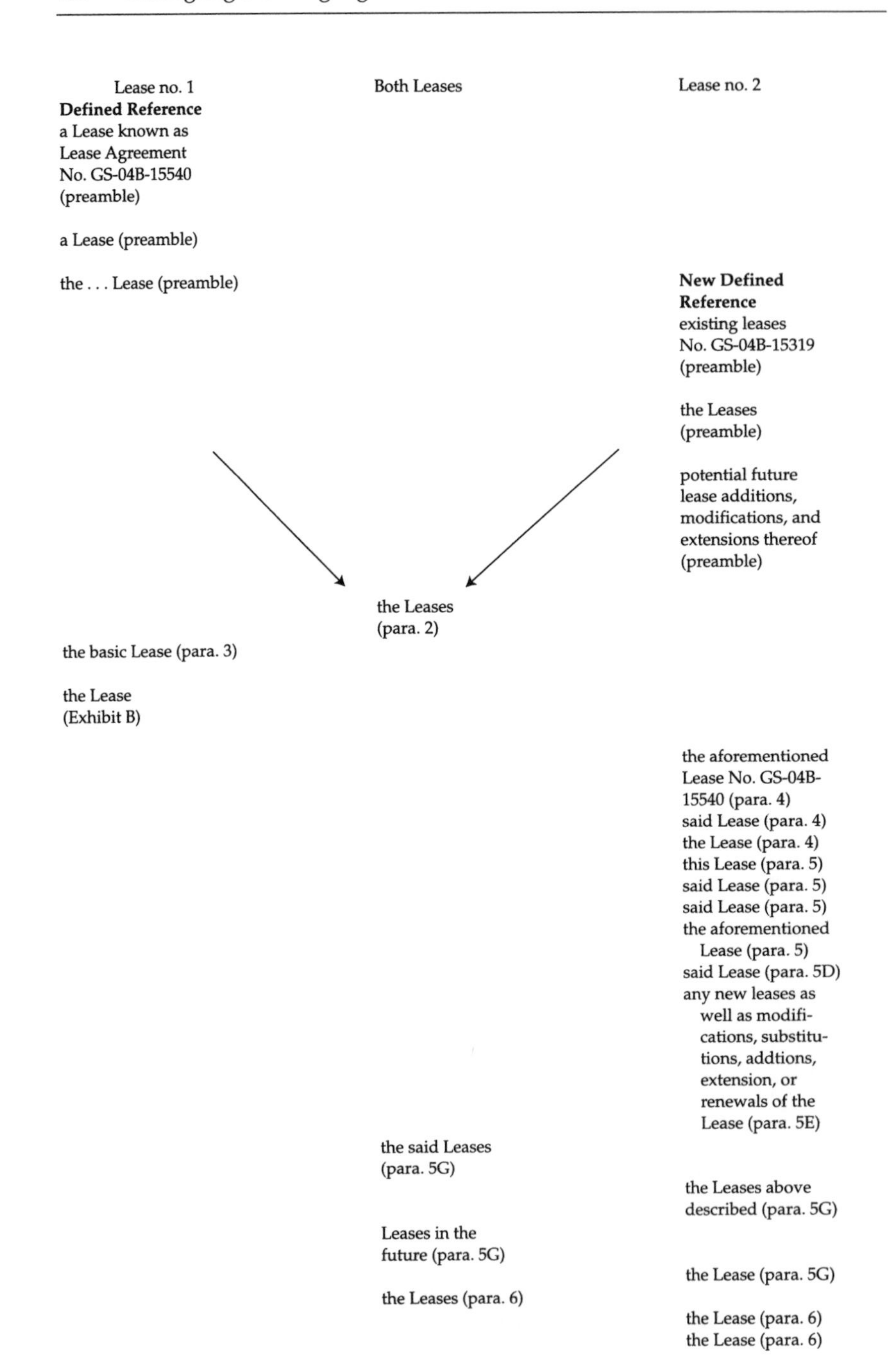

FIGURE 7-7. Lease References (Agreement Three)

that of the rest of the document. As in the other commission agreements, this reference to "Lease" is defined by the property to which it refers.

The significance of this referencing and to property and lease for property in Commission Agreement No. 3 is as follows. It shows that all references to property up to paragraph ten are to the property defined in Exhibit A, and that all references to lease or leases up to paragraph ten relate only to that property. It also shows clearly that in paragraph ten, a newly defined property reference is the existing Waterford Plaza Building, 643 Denmark Avenue, and that all references to further or future lease or leases of that property, not relating to the U.S. Customs Service, are not commissionable to Mr. Green unless a separate written instrument is executed toward that end.

It should be further mentioned that there is, in Commission Agreement No. 3, one other reference to new leases (paragraph 5E). It is clear from the anaphoric reference in this document that this reference to "any new leases" is governed by the property reference to which it relates, in this case, the second lease (second defined reference, in the preamble), "existing leases No. GS-04B-15319," and not to any other property.

To this point we have described how anaphoric reference helps determine the specific references to property and lease(s) that relate to that property. In the three commission agreements it is possible, through much effort, to clarify the references, as noted above. There are, in all three documents, structural clues such as plural markers; article determination, such as "a" versus "the"; or specific terms used primarily by the legal and/or real estate profession, such as "said property," to produce complex but unambiguous referencing in these documents. Thus far, the linguistic tool employed was largely that of syntax analysis. In research, however, it is also useful to examine the data from different perspectives or approaches in order to validate or confirm the findings of one or more of the other approaches. Therefore, we subjected the data here to two further analyses, discourse analysis and contrastive analysis.

Discourse Analysis

As it turns out, discourse analysis offers further support for the syntactic findings. Topic-comment analysis of written and spoken discourse has rules quite parallel to the syntactic rules of anaphora. To introduce a topic, one must clearly identify or mark the substance of that topic. Likewise, once a topic has been changed to another topic, it is necessary to clearly mark or specify its reintroduction or recycling. For example, if one were writing about a specific piece of clearly identified property, it would be necessary to mark the change of that topic to something else. Then, if one wished to recycle discussion about the first piece of property, it would be necessary to clearly mark, through topic identification, this return to the original topic. As such, topic-comment analysis of discourse follows the same general rules as those of anaphoric referencing. That is, the topic, once clearly established, is expected to be unified and consistent unless or until clearly marked to the contrary. Such an analysis of the three commission agreements yields exactly the same results as the previous referencing analysis.

Commission Agreement No. 1 contains two types of topics: substantive topics and corollary topics (Shuy 1982). Substantive topics are ones which are the substantive reason for the existence of the document. Corollary topics serve the substantive topics by specifying how they will be accomplished (manner, conditions, amount of payment, etc.). This distinction between substantive and corollary is not qualitative or evaluative, since corollary topics can be important as well. The distinction is more one of function.

The substantive topic of Commission Agreement No. 1 is the relationship of certain property to a lease. The primary aspect is the property, since a lease is meaningless without clear identification with the property with which it connects. Thus, it is first necessary to identify the property before one specifies any lease related to it. The corollary topics are those which implement and provide procedures, conditions, and details for the substantive topic of the property-lease relationship.

The topic-comment analysis of this agreement is shown in Figure 7-8.

Substantive topic:	Comment:
Specific property plus specific lease	Exhibit A
Corollary topics:	
1. The preamble is true	
2. Mr. Green is sole broker	for the lease between owner and GSA
3. Time and amount of lease	10 years, $177,540 per year
4. Commission	10% of said Lease plus details of payment
5. Notification	where and how
6. Enforcement possibilities	enforcing party to be reimbursed if successful
7. Binding nature	heirs, successors, etc.
8. Exceptions to substantive topic	Waterford Plaza Building

FIGURE 7-8. Topic-Comment Analysis (Agreement One)

The significance of this analysis is that there is only one substantive topic of which all other topics are corollary. If there are any claims that changes were made in the substantive topic, such changes are unmarked in the structure of this discourse event and cannot be supported.

The substantive topic of Commission Agreement No. 2 is also the relationship of certain property to a lease as shown in Figure 7-9.

The significance of the analysis of this second agreement, as in the first agreement, is that there is only one substantive topic of which all other topics are corollary. If anyone wishes to claim that there are any changes made in this lone substantive topic, this analysis does not support such a claim.

As in Commission Agreement No. 1 and Commission Agreement No. 2, there is only one substantive topic in Commission Agreement No. 3. A

Substantive topic:	Comment:
Specific property plus specific lease	1. Exhibit A, together with entire water frontage bordering the property described herein
	2. Supplemental Lease
Corollary topics:	
1. Preamble is true	
2. Mr. Green is sole broker	of leases between Broker and GSA
3. Time and amount	10 years, $222,588 per year plus additional rental or compensation
4. Commission	10% Supplemental Lease plus any additional benefits. Parking space plus other details.
5. Event of sale or condemnation	commission plus details
6. Notification procedure	addresses
7. Enforcement possibilities	enforcing party to be reimbursed if successful
8. Binding nature	heirs, successors, etc.
9. Exception to substantive topic	Waterford Plaza Building

FIGURE 7-9. Topic Comment Analysis (Agreement Two)

major difference here is that this agreement deals with more than one lease, as shown in Figure 7-10.

Again, the analysis of this agreement shows that there is only one substantive topic, of which all other topics are corollary. If claims are made that there are changes in the meaning of the substantive topic, such claims are not supported by the structure of the discourse event. The rules of topic maintenance are clearly honored here. No newly marked substantive topic concerning property and lease (or any other new topic) is introduced.

Substantive topic:	Comment:
Specific property plus specific leases	Exhibit A Lease Agreement No. GS-04B-15540 and GS-04B-15319
Corollary topics:	
1. Preamble is true	
2. Mr. Green is sole broker	of leases between Owner and GSA
3. Time and amount	10 years, $271,576 per year
4. Options to renew	additional two 5-year periods
5. Commission	10% this Lease plus other compensation
6. Event of sale or condemnation	10% commission plus details
7. Notification procedure	addresses
8. Enforcement possibilities	enforcing party to be reimbursed if successful
9. Binding nature	
10. Exceptions to substantive topic	Waterford Plaza Building

FIGURE 7-10. Topic-Comment Analysis (Agreement Three)

Contrastive Analysis

The third analytical procedure used to validate or confirm earlier anaphoric referencing and discourse analysis is that of contrastive analysis. Contrastive analysis is a procedure used by scientists of virtually all disciplines to determine the unique structure of substances or events by displaying data in juxtaposition, in order to determine how much alike or unlike each other they are. The type of contrastive analysis performed on the three commission agreements is a contrastive analysis of what the documents say with what they do not say, in relation to the dispute in the case.

If it were the intention of the signers of these commission agreements to provide an exclusive agreement to the broker for commissions on all property owned currently and in the future by the owner and leased to the General Services Administration GSA (of course does not even address the issue of whether or not the lessor in question is GSA, the U.S. Customs Service, or any other federal department), there would be some indication of that intention, perhaps even a clear one, in these documents. From the previous analyses of referencing and topic-comment, it is clear that such indicators do not exist. If they were to exist, however, one might expect to find them in such places as this contrastive analysis points out. It should be noted that in both criminal and civil trials in which I have been asked to analyze the evidence, often what is **not** said or written turns out to be as important as what **was** said or written.

In Commission Agreement No. 1, the clearest place for the signers of these documents to have indicated that their intention was to provide an exclusive agreement between the lessor and the owner for a right to commission on all property, owned currently or in the future by the owner, would be in the property identification and the following referencing to it, especially in references to property that is not specifically subject to exclusion from commission to the broker.

In the first commission agreement, a golden opportunity for such a statement would be in the preamble, where the defined reference to the property is made:

What it says:	What it does not say:
the property more specifically set forth in Exhibit A attached hereto and made part hereof and together with the entire water frontage bordering on property described herein.	the property more specifically set forth in Exhibit A attached hereto and made a part hereof **and all other property currently owned by the OWNER LESSOR or purchased at any future date in any other location and leased to GSA**

If the agreement had contained these bolded words, instead of what it actually says, the broker could have made his case and the dispute might be ended. Commission Agreement No. 1 did not say this, however.

Almost exactly the same things could be said about the second and third commission agreements. Since all subsequent references to property are structurally explicit anaphoric references to Exhibit A, "together with the entire water frontage bordering the property described herein" (in the second agreement), or simply "Exhibit A" (in the third agreement), it is totally unfounded that what was intended by the signers was for all the property that the owner currently owned or all that he might purchase in the future should yield commissions to the broker.

The broker believed, somehow, that even though the initial, substantive topic reference to the property under discussion (initially identified in each of the preambles) was to the property described in Exhibit A, a later reference or later references to property actually opened the door to a broader definition of what the property really was. If this were the case, figure 7-11 would have been required:

Conclusion

As is evident from the documents themselves, there is no indication either in the initial substantive topic reference nor in any subsequent anaphoric reference that the signers of these documents intended the meaning of "property" to include, at any time, any property than that which was specified as Exhibit A "together with the entire water frontage bordering the property described herein" in Commission Agreements No. 1 and No. 2, or simply as Exhibit A in Commission Agreement No. 3. No language evidence is present to indicate, furthermore, that any subsequent anaphoric reference to the original defined reference was present or was intended. It should be made perfectly clear, though, that such linguistic analysis can make no claim about the actual intentions of the writers or signers of these documents, only that the actual language and structure of the discourse does not give evidence of such intentions.

Disputes in legal issues often revolve around the wording, syntax, or discourse structure of the language used. There are many tools available to linguists for analyzing such documents. In the case of these commission agreements, the three analytical routines selected (anaphora, topic analysis, and contrastive analysis) were chosen because they are the most appropriate for addressing this particular issue. The problem drives the selection of analytical routines to be used. This analysis, which also demonstrates that even the jargon-ridden and complex language of law and business is capable of being untangled, was instrumental in settling the dispute in favor of the owner.

What it says:	What it does not say:
in Commission Agreement No. 1	
in preamble:	
the property	this property and all other currently or future owned property
in preamble:	
said property	said property and all other currently or future owned property
Commission Agreement No. 2	
in preamble:	
the property	this property and all other currently or future owned property
in preamble:	
the said property	the said property and all other said currently or future owned property
in paragraph 4:	
the land specified	the land specified here and all other currently or future owned property
in paragraph 5:	
the within premises	the within premises and all other currently or future owned property
Commission Agreement No. 3	
in preamble:	
the property	this property and all other currently or future owned property
in preamble:	
real property	real property in this case and all currently or future owned property
in paragraph 6:	
the within premises	the within premises and all other currently or future owned property
in paragraph 6:	
the property	this property and all other currently or future owned property

FIGURE 7-11. Contrastive Analysis

Chapter 8

Attacking the Bureaucratic Language of Car Sales: A Case Study of a Car Sales Event

Many people express their discomfort with the car-buying event, but it has been difficult to document each painful step in the process. I have had the opportunity to review audio-taped documentation of car-buying episodes in various money laundering cases, where the buyer (actually an undercover law enforcement agent) goes through some of the usual steps of car purchasing. But such data are not really representative of the average car-buying event, since the presentations, first of all, were done by undercover police acting as buyers, and secondly, the police acted in the flamboyant and atypical manner that they believed might typify a drug dealer. One can also call on personal experiences buying cars, but memory of the exact details of each step in the process fade quickly, especially when the event was not particularly pleasant, and questions about the awkwardness, inappropriateness, and even legality of taping such events easily discourages such documentation. Alternatively one could, I suppose, utilize the participant observation technique from inside the business by getting oneself hired as a car salesman and then describing in detail the everyday events for a period of time. Needless to say, this suggestion was not very appealing.

The following description of the bureaucracy of car sales is based on an unusual event in which evidence of the various steps in a car sales process were memorialized for later analysis. It should be made perfectly clear, however, that not all aspects or actions of this recorded event, particularly the most egregious ones, should be generalized to all car dealers. It is the basic, common outline that we focus on here.

Background

It appeared that there would be no easy way to capture the inner workings of the car sales bureaucracy until, in 1987, a Fort Worth attorney, Michael Johnson, called me about a most unusual case. His client was a young adult named Mitchell Bien, who had come to him with a complaint about a local car dealership. Johnson did not normally take cases such as this but as Bien unfolded his story, Johnson was stunned by the violations of human rights that his client revealed.

Getting the client's story is the attorney's first task. This is difficult enough to do when the client is articulate, but Bien posed a further complication: he had been deaf from birth. He was raised by hearing parents but his father had died recently, leaving his car to his son. Although many deaf people become quite independent in the hearing world, Bien had not. He had depended on his father to be his translator and to aid in his transactions with the hearing world. This trip to the car dealer was one of Bien's first independent ventures into this wider world. After his unhappy, if not traumatic, experience trying to price a new vehicle, Bien thought he had been treated badly enough to see a lawyer about a lawsuit.

As attorney Johnson wondered what sort of evidence might support Bien's claim of maltreatment, his client pulled out a stack of 101 four-by-four inch pieces of paper, covered with handwriting. Closer examination revealed that the writing was in three different hands. Then Johnson realized that even in this very interview, he had been communicating with his client by exchanging notes, and that the 101 pieces of paper produced by Bien could be, in essence, like a tape recording of Bien's experience with the car dealership.

The attorney quickly examined the notes but could not find any logical sequence to them. Although Bien and the salesman had written notes to each other, there was, of course, no reason to have numbered the exchanges or sequenced the pieces of paper while their written communication took place. So the evidence, if it were to be useful as a record of what took place, needed to be put together in the way that the event actually unfolded.

Attorney Johnson worked with his client to try to sequence the papers and finally presented the results in their law suit (Tarrant County, No. 348-111259-88), which charged the dealership with negligence, gross negligence, false imprisonment, infliction of emotional distress, fraud, violations of the state's Deceptive Trade Practices Act, and violations of the Texas Human Resources code's protection of the handicapped. The defendants challenged this sequence, noting that if the exchanges were arranged in a different order, the result would be totally different story of what happened. What Johnson needed, then, was a linguistic analysis that would either verify or correct the sequence that his client reported. He thought that the language itself might provide such clues. So he called me.

My analysis of the writing on the notes ultimately confirmed, with minor modifications, Bien's view of the order of their written exchanges. And I testified to this at trial, showing how I went about my analysis. I reported this in an article in *Forensic Linguistics* (Shuy 1994). Bien prevailed in court and was awarded a large sum of money by the jury. However, the details of that particular case are of less concern here than the present focus on the bureaucratic language of the automobile sales business, as revealed by this evidence. The notes provided a fascinating picture of that bureaucracy.

Bureaucratic language, as has been noted throughout this book, is characterized by specialized functions, adherence to fixed rules, a hierarchy of authority, and an administrative system marked by officialism, red tape, and proliferation. These characteristics frame the following analysis of the car sales bureaucracy.

Specialization of Functions

A car dealership, like virtually any business, has specialized roles and functions. There are the usual secretaries, typists, mechanics, and lower-level positions. Then there are the salespersons, managers, and other layers of bosses. The function of a salesperson is fairly obvious: to sell products to customers. The function of a car salesperson is more complex, however, and since the sale involves a very large amount of money, customers are more reluctant to bite. To encourage purchases, car salespersons proceed methodically in six predictable phases, which I describe in my earlier analysis of this case (Shuy 1994). In order to be able to identify the specialized functions of the salesperson, it is first necessary to determine the general sequential phases in the sales event. This is important because the specialized functions vary throughout the sales event and these different phases cannot replace or substitute for each other. Nor can they be presupposed if and when they do not explicitly exist, especially in a significant financial transaction such as the purchase of a car. Therefore, it is also useful to identify these phases to contextualize the bureaucratic functions that occur within them. The significance of whether or not an offer was presented by the salesperson and a counter offer was ever made and/or accepted by the customer framed the controversy in this lawsuit.

A car sales event begins with (1) greetings and introductions, followed by (2) presenting and/or ascertaining needs, moves next to (3) a display of the product, which then leads to (4) making an offer and negotiation, (5) a completion of the transaction, and finally to (6) the closing. These are sequenced phases, as follows:

1. Greetings and Introductions Phase

It is typical that a prospective customer enters the dealership and wanders around a bit, examining the cars in the showroom or on the adjacent lot. Salespersons appear to let them do this for a while, then eventually approach them, identify themselves, shake hands, and offer them a warm welcome as well as some sort of hospitality, such as soft drinks or coffee.

2. Needs Phase

After the greeting and introduction, the car sales event requires salespersons to determine the needs of the customer. This enables them to focus on the appropriate model, style, color, and extras of the product, as a precursor to showing the product, and ultimately to making an offer. The salespersons' function is to try to narrow the focus as much as possible in order to save time and effort. They attempt to avoid any talk about cost at this time since they want to build up the customer's desire level to the point where future negotiations about cost will work in favor of the salesperson. If a customer should ask about price during this phase, the salesperson gives a very broad range of prices, not specific ones, saving preciseness for the later negotiation part of the "Make Offer" phase.

Another specialized function of the salesperson is to assess the customer's available resources, a tricky thing to do. In terms of sales technique, such information is better obtained once customers are so excited about a specific model that they are numb to such personal probing. But since such excitement is often useless if the salesperson ultimately discovers that they cannot afford the model or are not eligible for a suitable loan, the "customer profile" often begins rather generally and broadly during the "Needs" phase, so that such facts are casually gathered as early as possible without appearing to pry.

3. Display Product Phase

After the customers' needs become fairly clear, the salesperson begins to show them various models. This usually culminates with a test drive. This phase is structured to cause the customer to want the product even more. To this point, the desire for the car has been abstract; now it becomes physically real. The salesperson now displays not only the car, but also the qualities of the manufacturer, the dealership, the service department, the sales force, and even the individual salesperson. Hospitality, such as a cup of coffee and donuts, is a common part of this phase.

4. Make Offer Phase

This phase is often foreshadowed during the "Display Product" phase, especially if things seem to be going well for the salesperson. It is common for the salesperson to introduce this phase with words such as, "When would you like to take delivery?" even though no agreement to purchase has been made. Such words presuppose agreement and permit easy transition into the more complex money discussion that follows. Specific prices for specific cars are given in this phase. The "customer profile" is now pursued in earnest, completing any information that had been started only informally or broadly to this point. It is common for the salesperson to bring out a standard offer form to record such information on paper, accompanied by the customer's signature. This strategy will be treated later in the bureaucratic component of adherence to fixed rules. Equally common is for salespersons to make offers that request a higher price or trade-in equivalent than they expect to be able to get. Such a strategy puts many American buyers at a disadvantage, since bartering is not common in this country in most commercial contexts. This fact is not wasted on some automobile salespersons.

The expectation, or at least the opportunity, then exists for customers to make a counter offer. If customers are savvy enough to know that this is the expected reaction, they can make one. If no counter offer is made, the salesperson can assume that customers are satisfied with the offer, even though this may not be the case, or that they may simply not understand the bartering procedure. In any case, the salesperson can also suggest that customers make a counter offer (although the term, "counter," is seldom used), especially if there seems to be no response at all to the salesperson's original offer, or if the customer appears to react negatively, even though non-verbally, to that offer. Both the offer and any counter offers count only when they are both explicit and unconditional. "I might be able to get this car for you for $18,000" is a conditional effort, not a legitimate offer. Likewise, "I might buy if you give me $5,200 on a trade-in" does not constitute a counter offer, since it is couched in the conditional.

The "Make Offer" phase is one in which negotiation can take place, not just about the price of the car, but also about trade-in value, accessories, and other issues. Again, salespersons are usually at an advantage here, simply because this is their business and they are practiced at it while customers usually are not. It is common, nevertheless, for salespersons to compliment customers on their shrewd negotiation skills, even when there is little or no evidence of any. The negotiation may well take on a further complexity. At some point, especially when the salesperson is forced to give in a bit to the customer's wishes, the proposal suddenly must meet the approval of the salesperson's boss. This situation will be dealt with as evidence of the bureaucratic component, "hierarchy of authority."

5. Complete Transaction Phase

When the customer unconditionally agrees to buy the car at the price agreed to by the agency, the transaction is completed, usually accompanied by a verbal agreement and a signed contract. Without such as unconditional, formalized agreement, there is no completion of the deal.

6. Closing Phase

This is a time of pleasantness, relief, and once again, hospitality and congratulations. For the dealership, it is an opportunity to make customers feel that they did the right thing and to convince them that they would be wise to continue to buy there in the future and to make use of the dealership's service department. One American brand of automobiles has instituted a ritual in which all salespersons and staff come together and sing their congratulations to the new buyer.

There can be no question that the car sales event is a product of many specialized functions, and that each of these is located in a proper sequence. Like most bureaucratic events, the outsider to the bureaucracy is more or less unfamiliar with these special functions and is, consequently, disadvantaged by them. Although other sales events, such as buying a diamond ring, may contain similar unfamiliarities, the car sales event has the added disadvantage of high economic consequences and is, at the same time, fraught with distrust and mixed emotions.

Adherence to Fixed Rules

There are, of course, fixed rules that any dealership must follow. As has been noted in other chapters in this book, the difficult characteristic of bureaucracies is not that there are rules, but that the representation of these rules is often oppressive and carried out in ways that appear to protect the agency more than they serve the public.

At a point during the "Make Offer" phase, the salesperson brought out what is called, in this case, "Computerized Price & Equipment Confirmation." This was a printed form, one page long, reproduced as Figure 8-1.

Once the salesperson believed that he had found the car that the customer was interested in, he brought out this form, a first step in the "Make Offer" phase. He had previously asked the customer's name, address, and Social Security Number, so that when the form was presented to Bien,

COMPUTER PRICE & EQUIPMENT CONFIRMATION

(customer's name, address and social security number)	STOCK NO.: ______ DEAL NO.: ______ SALESMAN: ______ DATE: ______
VEHICLE DESCRIPTION NISSAN 300ZX RED TM1HZ 14S3HX201018	SELLING PRICE: 20,977.00 CURRENT MARKET VALUE ______ LESS RECONDITIONING ______ BUYERS ALLOWANCE ______
1302 WIDE BODY SIDE MOLD 350 PIN STIPES 80 MAKE/READY-STATE INS 0245 T-TOP ENGRAVING 82 STATE INSPECTION 02 SECURITY SYS PROGSV	DIFFERENCE ______ PAYOFF ______ CASHDOWN ______ PAYMENTS ______

The selling price does not include sales tax, title, transfer registration, state inspection or documentary fees.

Credit Check Release
Please sign and give us your Social Security Number to authorize us to apply for a credit check.

________________ your signature please   ________________ SSN:

FIGURE 8-1. Computer Price & Equipment Confirmation

these were already typed in, along with the specifics of the vehicle description, equipment, stock number, deal number, date, and salesman's name. The document, when presented to Bien, looked very official and orderly. Although there is no evidence from the notes that a long pause took place previous to this point, there could be no other explanation for the form's having this information typed in. It looked very official and bureaucratically proper.

In terms of bureaucratic language, note first the title, "Computer Price & Equipment Confirmation." Although the form does indeed speak to price and equipment, there is nothing in the title to suggest that an offer had been made or, in fact, that the form was in any way intended to memorialize an offer or counter offer. The use of the word, "Computer," in the title adds to its official, bureaucratic appearance, even though there is little if anything about the form that suggests computerization. The word, "Confirmation," is also interesting in that it is vague about what or who is confirming what. It certainly "confirms" which vehicle is being looked at. Does it also suggest that Bien is confirming that he wanted to buy it? The dealership thought so and testified to this at trial. When something is confirmed, however, it is useful, if not absolutely necessary, to state clearly what the confirmation refers to and who is doing the confirming. The form fails in both respects.

"Current Market Value," "Less Reconditioning," and "Buyers Allowance" refer to trade-in. When Bien had driven up to the dealership, it was clearly apparent that he had a vehicle. As the notes make clear, Bien expressed no intention of buying a car that day. He explained that he came in there to find out the general parameters of what a new car might cost if at some time he might decide to buy one. Many potential customers begin in this way and salespersons naturally try to speed the process along by convincing customers that they need look no further for the car of their dreams.

Since he had seen Bien's vehicle, the salesperson asked Bien if his plans included considering a trade-in if and when he might make a purchase. Since he saw no reason not to, Bien consented when asked for his car keys so that the appraiser might examine his car. Again the dealership argued that this information indicated that Bien indeed had begun the negotiation part of the "Make Offer" phase, even though, in his words, he had only consented to this as a matter of information and not as an indication of any negotiation or commitment to buy a car. That these figures were the product of the dealership, and not those of Bien, seem to be confirmed by what was handwritten on the form after the categories, "Payoff" and "Payments." Inked in was "10,000 and 36 @ 330–345 mo." The note indicates that at no time did Bien indicate that he had that much money to put down, or that he requested the amount of monthly payments of any kind.

The salesperson simply skipped this matter, much as he did when he asked earlier, "When would you like to accept delivery?" If some car salespersons can move a sale along by presupposing the past move, even though it never actually occurred, the eventual sale can be speeded up, but the validity of the move may well be questioned if there is no explicit agreement to it.

When he was shown this form, Bien objected to the small trade-in value that was handwritten on the form, "3,879.00, less conditioning, 879." "Buyers allowance" was inked in as "3,000." Before the salesperson left Bien alone and went to have the form filled out, Bien had written, "I don't think to buy new because it is too expensive." Undaunted by this, the salesperson went ahead with the form, claiming that he had to get authorization from his boss. Upon seeing the form, Bien objected, writing "Almost half price lose, not worth. Last May bought it for 5,775. Now 3,000." The salesperson replied, "This is best offer," to which Bien wrote, "If I buy new and I still lose $2,575 for my truck."

Missing from the dealership's interpretation of these written exchanges is the conditionality of Bien's preceding exchanges, full of "if's," expressions of his intention only to shop for prices, and his clear declarations that he wanted his keys back because he wanted to leave. The salesperson ignored Bien's pleas.

As in much of the bureaucratic language described in this book, the bureaucratic rules that were apparently guiding the salesperson in this case were not made explicitly or clearly. Nor was there any authorization from the customer to go to the next phase of the transaction. The Computer Price & Equipment Confirmation form may have been clear enough to the dealership, but the customer's perspective was not taken into account (it is possible, of course, that the dealership intended to deliberately mask its intention to the customer).

In governmental bureaucracies that exist as a result of acts of Congress and are set up for the purpose of serving the public, there is a growing understanding that the public's perspective must be taken into account. In commercial business, taking the customer's perspective appears to be a bit less strongly felt. There is a strong need to attract the public, convince it to buy the product, and, in some good businesses, a need to be of service to the consumer. Taking the consumer's perspective with regard to the language used, however, is still often in its infancy, as evidenced by the language found on the warning labels of many commercial products, on assembly instructions for children's' toys, in advertisements, and on many other things.

Most commercial advertisements offer little or no information about the product, preferring only to gain product recognition in the ads. In the case of the car sales event, giving at least some information is central to the salesperson's effort to determine the customer's needs and to narrow the options available. In the current case, information about the sales event itself, such as whether or not an offer was made, and whether or not the customer had made a counter offer signaling that he was actually into the negotiation process, was badly obscured in the ways noted above.

By adhering to the fixed rules of presenting the "Computerized Price & Equipment Confirmation" form at the time and in the way it was presented, the salesperson was probably following standard car sales procedure, at least for this dealership. In fact, at trial, others in the dealership testified that this was, indeed, the case. The salesman should not be penalized, they argued, since this is how they claimed that the sales event was conventionally carried out. In short, the dealership tried to hide behind what they portrayed as the fixed rules of the bureaucratic wall.

Hierarchy of Authority

It was noted above that just before the "Computer Price & Equipment Confirmation" form was brought out, the salesperson disappeared for an unknown length of time. Leaving the customer alone like this is recommended in some training programs for car salespersons, as was brought out in trial. This is done to intensify the customer's desire for the car and to make him want to get the transaction over with even if he has to give in on the matter of price. Bien spent at least four hours in the dealership, even though his purpose from the outset, as his written notes reveal, was only to price a car for some later possible purchase. Evidence of the time lapse can be found on the notes' references to time throughout, such as "I have been here for two/three hours, so I'm tired now."

To his presupposed question, "When do you want to take delivery?" the salesman got no response, at least none that was written on the notes. He then asked Bien to make a counter offer. Receiving no response again, the salesperson began the conventional car sales role switch, familiar to most of us in our car buying experience. He now became Bien's ally, writing, "Let me work on my manager," placing the manager in the opposition role. Like most bureaucracies, there is always an appeal to some higher authority, often abstract, distant, or even absent.

Before the salesperson left Bien in the cubicle, he wrote, "If I can get you a better deal would you finance or pay cash? Give me some help. I need to show my boss some form of money. Cash, credit card, check, anything. Help me. My sharp buyers use a portion of their money to dangle in front of my boss to get a good deal! I need a check for $4,000 to use as negotiating leverage to use against my boss. I'll give it back. Write me a check for $4,000 so I can bring it to my boss to try to get this deal." Bien wrote back,

"If good deal and I will call my insurance then come back here." Bien wrote a check, perhaps feeling at last that someone was finally on his side in this affair. In doing so, of course, he played into the hands of the dealership, for they could now use this as evidence that he had indeed wanted to buy a car at that time. But again the dealership forgot to consider that Bien had written five previous exchanges that began with "if":

- "If your boss accept I can't buy it right now."
- "If I write my check then you will return it back."
- "If good deal I will call my insurance."
- "If good deal then go to home and call my insurance for how much cost for that car."
- "If your boss accept I can't buy it right now so rather talking my insurance man."

Bien's consistent goal was to determine how much all this would cost and not to purchase anything that day.

The salesperson protected his relationship with Bien by not taking responsibility for the figures on the "Computerized Price & Equipment Confirmation" form. He was now joined with Bien in a contest with the bureaucratic hierarchy, the good guy–bad guy routine so common in police interrogations of suspects. The next step was to get Bien happy with the boss by creating still another, more abstract enemy. The salesman, noting Bien's displeasure with the figures on the form, wrote: "Why don't you like my boss?" To this, Bien replied, "because he gave me too high Price and lose my money for truck in price." To this, the salesperson wrote, "Don't get mad at my boss. These are buyer's figures." Now there was still another higher authority that both the salesman and the boss could not do anything about, another level in the bureaucratic hierarchy. This level was not assailable, however, since the buyer was a person, real or imagined, who was not present and was not to be present. In essence, the salesperson and the boss (who eventually appeared and wrote a few exchanges but who turned out, in reality, to be just another salesman) were allegedly on Bien's side but were hopelessly trapped in a bureaucracy where nothing could be done, since authority was out of their hands. This is a familiar cry of people who complain about "the bureaucracy." There is always some higher level that cannot be reached.

Administration of Officialdom, Red Tape and Proliferation

One of the most frustrating aspects of bureaucracies is the red tape and waiting they inflict upon outsiders. We have already noted that Bien was kept waiting various times throughout some four hours that he spent in the dealership. On the eighty-second note sheet, Bien complains, "I have been here for two three hours so I'm tired now." On the ninety-fifth note sheet he writes, "You can't hold me to stay here too long for 4 hours because I already been here for 4 hours." Each note sheet contained at least one written exchange and sometimes two or three, so it is clear that long intervals existed between exchanges.

Bureaucracies are also often accused of giving clients the run-around even when responding to relatively simple requests. In note forty-three, the salesperson asks Bien for a check, and it is clear that by note forty-nine this check had been written and given to the salesperson. After a wait, the "Computerized Price & Equipment Confirmation" sheet emerges and Bien begins a series of statements about wanting to leave. He is disappointed at the boss's suggested trade-in value and, on note fifty-nine, makes the first of a series of requests to get his check back, as follows:

59 Bien: Please return my check now and I have gone now because my brother looking at me too long.
60 Bien: Please return my check now!
Salesman: Don't give up till I give up.
75 Bien: Where is my check?
Salesman: It is safe. In the desk office.
77 Bien: Please listin me, please return by check now because I'm little pressure myself. Please let me go home for rest.
78 Bien: Where is your boss's office and I have get my check back.
79 Bien: You are Liar because you say you will bring it back after your boss see it but you won't bring it back.
Salesman: I thought we were friends!
82 Bien: Tell your boss, please return my check now!
Salesman: Why?
83 Bien: Please bring it back Now or drive to Police dept.
Salesman: The police want you to buy a new car and get a good deal!
89 Bien: Show me where is your boss's office.
90 Bien: If you won't show his office then go straight to police dept. or
Salesman: My boss is coming out to meet you!

The pattern of the salesperson's responses offer insights into the car sales use of bureaucratic language. To Bien's requests on notes 59, 77, 78 and 89, the salesperson gives no answer at all. His answer to sixty is off topic, "Don't give up till I give up." It presumes that Bien's earlier requests to get his check back are not serious and that Bien's earlier statements that he is not there to buy are unbelievable. Not only does the salesperson demean Bien in this way, but he fails totally to take Bien's perspective. To Bien's request to learn where his check is, the salesperson tells him that it is safe in the boss's office, ignoring the intent of Bien's continuous meaning that he wants it back. To Bien's complaint that the salesperson had not kept his promise to give the check back, the salesman gratuitously offers that he thought they were friends. When Bien asks that he tell the boss to give it back, the salesman asks why, putting the customer in the frustrating position of knowing that whatever he says won't be listened to.

The *piece de resistance,* however, comes after Bien threatens to contact the police (83) and the salesperson treats Bien like a child, saying that the police want him to buy the car. Bien's second threat to call the police seems to call for drastic action. The alleged manager emerges, although in truth he is just another salesman working in consort with the first one. The remainder of the exchanges are reproduced as follows:

Salesman: My boss is coming out to meet you!
Manager: I'm the manager. Are you doing fine today!
Bien: I know you both push me to buy but I don't accept your deal!
Manager: I understand! That's why I came out personally to meet you. I want to save us both some time. What will you take right now for our truck?
Bien: I'm already little crazy man because you both held me to stay.
Manager: I just called the General Manager. He wants to know will you buy right now at your figures?
Bien: You can't hold me to stay here too long for four hours because I already been here for four hours. Please give me my check Right now.
Manager: Then let me go to our buyer to try one last time to get your figure.
Bien: Please gave me my check back NOW or . . .
Manager: Just one more second. We are close to putting a deal together. I need your understanding and need for you to be just a little flexible. 19,500 for our car. 3,200 buyers allowance I can sell mine with a discount but I cannot help that the used car market is so slow.

This ended the written exchanges. The last six statements of the "manager" were written on separate sheets of paper with no written responses from Bien. The series of verbal exchanges speaks for itself, but it might be noted that the appeal to authority seems to spiral here. The good guy–bad guy routine, common in police interrogations, again was pushed a step higher. This time the "manager" brings up the general manager and, once again, the buyer, as clogs in the bureaucratic machinery. The ploy is obviously to get Bien on their side by showing that they are on his, a common strategy in the car sales bureaucracy. In employing this strategy, the dealership displayed red tape, officialdom, and proliferation equal to that of any governmental bureaucracy.

Conclusion

I make no claim that the unfortunate experience of Mitchell Bien in his effort to find out the price of a car is common in all car sales. One would hope, in fact, that it is an aberration. But Bien's experience has a ring of familiarity about it to most people who have heard of this case, including the judge who, after the trial was over and the jury had awarded Bien a very large sum of money, told me that it was a fascinating "anatomy of a car sale." If this is typical of the car sales bureaucracy, things are even worse than one might imagine.

Chapter 9

Bureaucratic Language and Product Warning Labels: Case Studies of the Requirements of FDA and OSHA

Bureaucratic Language and Warnings

There was a time when manufacturers could content themselves with singing the praises of their products on their labels and in their advertisements. These days are gone. Government regulations, spurred on by consumer advocacy groups and, perhaps, an unusual sense of morality, now cause these manufacturers to convey warnings about the possible dangers of their products, or the use thereof, on their packaging. Just how these warnings are communicated opens the door to still another insight into bureaucratic language and how it is sent and received.

Product liability litigation is usually based on negligence, breach of warranty or strict liability in tort. Negligibility is somewhat obvious: the manufacturer causes unreasonable risk to the consumer by not exercising reasonable care in manufacturing or marketing the product. If the product did not do what the manufacturer claimed it would do, the issue is breach of warranty. Interestingly enough, breach of warranty includes problems which may not even be included in the warranty, usually found in the instructions about the use of the product. This is called implied warranty. Strict liability in tort relates to defective products, even if the manufacturer was not negligent and did not even know about the defect or make any claims about its performance.

For a product liability suit to succeed, there must be injury or damages which are caused by the product, there must be a defect in the product, and this defect had to be present when the product left the manufacturer's control. Product defects include not only faulty products themselves, but also faulty marketing, including warning labels.

Different government agencies have different requirements for warning labels, but they tend to hold in common that such labels must warn about all risks present in the product, do so adequately, and give adequate instructions for the use of the product. Adequate warnings must identify the seriousness of the risk, describe its nature, advise the consumer how to avoid it, and clearly communicate it.

Before manufacturers produce a warning label to accompany their products, they study the governmental requirements and standards. For example, the American National Standards Institute (ANSI), under the direction of the National Safety Council, produces standards for various industries as a guide to manufacturers, consumers, and the general public. These standards guide the manufacturer's writers as they produce hazard alert messages.

The ANSI standards committee adopted a three-level hazard alert system with the words, "Danger," "Warning," and "Caution." ANSI Z535 defines these terms as follows: "DANGER indicates an imminently hazardous situation which, if not avoided, *will* result in death or serious injury." "WARNING indicates a potentially hazardous situation which, if not avoided, *could* result in death or serious injury." "CAUTION indicates a hazardous situation which, if not avoided, *may* result in minor or moderate injury" (italics added). The difference between the imminence of "danger" and the potentiality of "warning" is significant. In addition, ANSI notes that "NOTICE" is to be used for hazards that can result only in property damage and "IMPORTANT" should be used as operating or maintenance suggestions. These definitions are significant in the analysis of the cases that follow here.

Bureaucratic Language and the U.S. Food and Drug Administration

An example of a federal regulation governing warnings to be provided by manufacturers of tampons is illustrative. The relevant part of this instruction put forth by the U.S. Food and Drug Administration (FDA) (Part 801.430) is as follows:

(b) Available data show that toxic shock syndrome (TSS), a rare but serious and sometimes fatal disease, is associated with the use of menstrual tampons. To protect the public and to minimize the serious adverse effects of TSS, menstrual tampons shall be labeled as set forth in paragraphs (c) and (d) in this section.

(c) If the information specified in paragraph (d) of this section is to be included as a package insert, the following alert statement shall appear prominently and legibly on the package label. ATTENTION: Tampons are associated with Toxic Shock Syndrome (TSS). TSS is a rare but serious disease that may cause death. Read and save the enclosed information.

(d) The consumer information required by this section shall appear prominently and legibly, in a package insert or on the package, in terms understandable by the layperson, and shall include statements concerning:

(1) (i) warning signs of TSS, e.g., sudden fever (usually 102° or more) and vomiting, diarrhea, fainting or near fainting when standing up, dizziness, or a rash that looks like a sunburn; (ii) what to do if these or other signs of TSS appear, including the need to remove the tampon at once and seek medical attention immediately;

(2) THE RISK OF TSS TO ALL WOMEN USING TAMPONS . . . especially the higher reported risks to women under 30 and teenage girls . . . and the risk of death from contracting TSS;

(3) the advisability of using tampons with the minimum absorbency needed . . .

(4) avoiding the risk of getting . . . TSS by not using tampons and . . . by alternating tampon use with sanitary napkin use . . .

(5) the need to seek medical attention before again using tampons if TSS warning signs have occurred . . . or if women have any questions about TSS or tampon use.

The above regulations were written to manufacturers, of course, and were not intended to be a word-for-word template for manufacturers to use in their warnings to consumers. But here is where some of the manufacturers' problems with lawsuits begin. It is clear that the intent of FDA regulation 801.430 is for manufacturers to instruct consumers that there is an association between tampon use and TSS and that a consumer takes a risk if she uses tampons. This is hard medicine for manufacturers to swallow since, by following the regulation explicitly, they may well scare away their prospective customers. The FDA does not specify the exact wording of most of this warning statement, but it is explicit about the content of what is to be warned, and about the requirement for prominence, legibility, and comprehensibility in wording this to the average consumer.

It is also interesting that the FDA regulations do not require that this information be captioned with the word, "Warning." The FDA refers to the required text as an "alert" statement that must use the word, "ATTENTION." On the other hand, the regulations do require the manufacturer to "warn" about the signs and dangers of TSS, although there is no explicit requirement to warn about the product itself.

"Alert" and "Attention" can both be located within the semantic network of "Warning," but not at the nodes of meaning where potentially bad or harmful things may happen. One does not warn about a potentially good eventuality, whereas one can alert a person or request a person's attention to either a good or bad event. Typical dictionary definitions define "warning" with words such as "attention" and "alert," and they define "alert" with the word, "warning."

To show how these terms interact, the following semantic network shown in Figure 9-1 may be helpful.

1. **Attention describes**	+ bad event + good event
2. **Alert describes**	+ bad event + good event

3. **Warning describes**	**Attention**	+ bad event + good event
	Alert	+ bad event + good event

FIGURE 9-1. Semantic Network of Warning Terms

Thus, even though the FDA requirements do not require manufacturers of tampons to caption their information with the word, "Warning," it is obviously illogical to warn about good events. Furthermore, both the words, "alert" and "attention," being semantic nodes of the word, "warning," have the capacity for referencing bad events. In truth, the consumer is to be warned, even though the required terms specify "alert" and "attention" here. It appears that the FDA dances around requiring captions that might offend the manufacturers.

This bureaucratic evasiveness may well stem from the process by which regulations are ultimately worded. FDA first puts out its intended regulations, then holds meetings in which manufacturers' representatives can make objections and suggest changes. The natural self-protectiveness of the manufacturers can easily come into play and lead to compromises in wording. FDA's choice of the more manufacturer-friendly terms, "alert" and "attention," are possibly the result of such compromise. FDA, on the other hand, could not require wording such as, "tampons will cause serious injury or death," for there is no reason to believe that these events will happen in all cases. Extensive research, cited in the regulations, has shown that there is, in fact, only a small chance of this happening. The same research has shown, in addition, that some people contact TSS without even having used tampons. The problem of the appropriate caption, then, appears to have been debatable, possibly leading to the FDA's decision not to insist on the word, "warning."

The issue of which word to use in the caption illustrates one aspect of bureaucratic language at work. For one thing, it shows that the government bureaucracy is capable of being influenced. Its hierarchy of authority comes face-to-face with that of the manufacturers in a contest of authoritative power reminiscent of the clash described earlier between the bureaucracies of Medicare and the medical profession. What is significant about the potential influence on the government's bureaucratic language here is that it does not reach down to the level of the consumer. The governmental bureaucracy solicits the advice of the manufacturing bureaucracy, but not normally that of the people for whom the product is intended.

To see how this compromise of the two bureaucracies plays out in real life, consider the case shown in Figure 9-2. In the late eighties and early nineties, tampon manufacturers attempted to comply with FDA regulations with package inserts such as the following (note that all print style and design is very close to the original and the manufacturer's name has been replaced by "X").

The obvious thing to do here is to compare the FDA requirements with the package insert, to see whether or not these requirements were satisfied. I have been called by attorneys to do this in various cases involving TSS in the past few years. In order to protect the anonymity of the parties involved in these cases, no real names will be used here.

Important Information About Toxic Shock Syndrome (TSS)

READ AND SAVE THIS INFORMATION ABOUT THESE TAMPONS:

WARNING SIGNS

WARNING SIGNS OF TSS FOR EXAMPLE ARE: SUDDEN FEVER (USUALLY 102° OR MORE) AND VOMITING, DIARRHEA, FAINTING OR NEAR FAINTING WHEN STANDING UP, DIZZINESS, OR A RASH THAT LOOKS LIKE A SUNBURN.

IF THESE OR OTHER SIGNS OF TSS APPEAR, YOUR SHOULD REMOVE THE TAMPON AT ONCE, DISCONTINUE USE, AND SEE YOUR DOCTOR IMMEDIATELY.

There is a risk of TSS to all women using tampons during their menstrual period. TSS is a rare but serious disease that may cause death. The reported risks are higher to women under 30 years of age and teenage girls. The incidence of TSS is estimated to be between 6 and 17 cases of TSS per 100,000 menstruating women and girls per year.

You can avoid any possible risk of getting tampon-associated TSS by not using tampons. You can possibly reduce the risk of getting TSS during your menstrual period by alternating tampon use with sanitary napkin use and by using tampons with the minimum absorbency.

X makes Regular absorbency tampons for lighter flows and Super and Super Plus absorbencies for heavier flows

If you had warning signs of TSS in the past, you should check with your doctor before using tampons again.

Information about TSS on the package and in the insert are provided by X in the public interest and in accordance with the Food and Drug Administration (FDA) tampon labeling requirements. TSS is believed to be a recently identified condition caused by a bacteria called staphylococcus aureus. The FDA recognizes that TSS also occurs among nonusers of tampons.

If you have any questions about TSS or tampon use, you should check with your doctor.

See Other Side for Usage Instructions

FIGURE 9-2. **Tampons Warning Statement**

The manufacturer of the tampon product in this case followed the FDA requirements by including what it considered the required information in a package insert, which is found once the consumer opens the package. This insert contains printed information on both sides. One side contains instructions on how to use the product (for a complete analysis of this information, see Shuy 1990). The other side is headed, "Important Information about Toxic Shock Syndrome (TSS)." Note here that the FDA regulations had specified that the word, "Attention," precede the caption and that the association of tampon use with TSS should be made clear in it. The manufacturer does neither in the caption, although such association can be found later in the text. There are nine information chunks in this part of the insert, as follows:

Information chunk	*Location, Print size*
1. Information about TSS	title, large print
2. Read and save this information	subtitle, all caps
3. Warning signs of TSS	title, all caps, paragraph 1
4. If warning signs, remove tampon	paragraph 2, all caps
5. Risk in using tampons of TSS	paragraph 3, lower case
6. How to avoid risk	paragraph 4, lower case
7. If past warning signs, see doctor	paragraph 5, lower case
8. a. This meets FDA requirements	paragraph 6, lower case
b. Tampons not the cause of TSS	paragraph 6, lower case
9. Any questions, see doctor	paragraph 7, lower case

Is the association between the use of tampons and TSS made? Yes. Is it made in a way that is understandable to the average consumer? Not likely. And this is the crux of most civil suits against tampon manufacturers. The self-protective and evasive manner in which this requirements is met is not uncommon in the bureaucratic language of manufacturers' warning statements. Since associating tampon use with TSS is the main purpose of this FDA requirement for the package insert alert statement, one might expect to find this association made earlier than in a dependent clause near the bottom of the first column. The adherence to fixed rules is preserved, but marginally at best. Interestingly enough, the manufacturer, in paragraph 6, cites the fact that FDA does not assert that tampon use is the sole cause of TSS. Although this is an accurate representation of the text found elsewhere in the FDA guidelines, it tends to defuse the sense of warning intended by the FDA in this warning statement. The letter of the law is kept, but the spirit is very weak. Attorneys for the manufacturer argued that the FDA requirement to associate tampon use with TSS was met. One has to agree with them. But these attorneys could not effectively support the claim that the insert's wording met the requirements of using "terms understandable by the layperson."

Even a cursory reading of the text here makes it clear that the main focus of the insert wording stresses the dangers of TSS, not the association of tampon use with TSS. The FDA requires prominence of this association. The insert words this as an adjective modifier, "tampon-associated TSS," well into the information—in a dependent clause, hardly prominent. Prominence is a notable aspect of document design, which is based on the principle that the purpose of the document dictates the design. The sequencing of information flows from the purpose. Both the language used and the shape or look of the document serve the sequencing purpose. If the document's purpose is to warn about an imminent danger, it should begin with such a warning and use clear and understandable words, syntax, and design. The package insert in question warns about TSS, but only weakly acknowledges the hazard of the association of TSS with tampon use.

In sharp contrast with the problems the Social Security Administration writers had in producing clear notices to beneficiaries (noted earlier in Chapter 2), the writers of this warning information could not claim to be simply ineffective in their efforts here. The other side of the warning information insert contained a tampon usage statement which provided clear evidence that the manufacturer's writers were quite competent to produce understandable information in a prominent way. The usage statement was clearly sequenced, and contained illustrations and bulleted statements that were clearly written. It contained an average of 9.4 words per sentence as opposed to the warning statement's 19.0 words per sentence. It contained far fewer dependent clauses and verbal compounds. It included sub-headings and half as many full lines of text. It had no more that two consecutive lines of all capital letters, as opposed to the warning statement's twelve consecutive lines of capitalized text.

If the writers were able to produce effective language in the usage section of the insert, why were they not able to do so in the warning statement? The ultimate answer, supported by the outcome of the trial, was that they chose not to or were instructed not to. The strong tendency of self-preservation probably led the company to try to disguise the dangers of such an association.

Once again, two bureaucracies bumped heads in a complex matter. In this case, competent advocacy of the woman suffering from TSS led to a decision in her favor, and it was the analysis of the bureaucratic language of both the FDA and the manufacturer that helped reach this decision.

Bureaucratic Language and the U.S. Occupational Safety and Health Administration (OSHA)

In another case involving warning statements, I was asked by attorneys to analyze the wording placed by the manufacturer of a very hazardous material for cleaning or removing oily substances, usually on boats. His client had suffered serious brain damage as a result of using this product (again, all names will be changed to maintain anonymity, as requested).

The American National Standards Institute's relevant regulations for this product were as follows (ANSI Z129.1):

> 3. General Requirements
>
> 3.1 The precautionary label for any hazardous chemical shall be based upon the hazards it possesses.
>
> 3.2 The following subject matter shall be considered for inclusion on precautionary labels: (1) identity of product or hazardous component(s), (2) signal word, (3) statement of hazards, (4) precautionary measures, (5) instructions in case of contact or exposure, (6) antidotes, (7) notes to physicians, (8) instructions in case of fire and spill or leak, and (9) instructions for container handling and storage.
>
> 3.3 Identification of the product or its hazardous chemical component(s) shall be adequate to permit selection of proper action in case of exposure. . . . Identification shall not be limited to non-descriptive code designation or trade name. If the product is a mixture, those chemicals (compounds) that contribute substantially to the hazard(s) shall be identified.
>
> 3.4 The *Signal Word* shall indicate the relative degree of severity of a hazard in the diminishing order of DANGER!, WARNING!, and CAUTION! When a product has more than one hazard, only the signal word corresponding to the class of the greatest hazard shall be used. . . .
>
> 3.6 The *Statement of Hazards* shall give notice of the hazard or hazards (such as EXTREMELY FLAMMABLE and HARMFUL IF ABSORBED THROUGH SKIN) that are present in connection with the customary or reasonably foreseeable handling or use of the product. With products possessing more that one such hazard, an appropriate statement for each significant hazard shall be included. In general, the most serious hazard shall be placed first. . . .
>
> 3.8 *Instructions in Case of Contact or Exposure* shall be included where the results of contact or exposure warrant immediate treatment (first aid), and where simple remedial measures may be taken safely before medical assistance is available. They shall be limited to procedures based on methods and materials com-

> monly available. Simple remedial measures (such as washing or removal of clothing) shall be included where they will serve to lessen or avoid serious injury following contact or exposure.
>
> 3.11 Antidotes that may be administered by a lay person shall be included on the label when applicable under the designation, *Antidote.* Antidotes that must be administered by a physician as well as other useful therapeutic measures, other than purely supportive treatment, shall be included on the label under the designation, *Note to Physicians.*

Manufacturers of hazardous materials, such as in this case, are required to file with the U.S. Department of Labor, Occupational Safety and Health Administration (OSHA), certain information required on a Material Safety Data Sheet (Form OSHA-20). This form should include all relevant information about the manufacturer, hazardous ingredients, physical data (boiling point, vapor pressure, solubility in water, specific gravity, percentage of volatility, evaporation rate), fire and explosion hazard data, health hazard data, reactivity data, spill or leak procedures, special protection information, and special precautions.

The manufacturer had filled out this form and under Section V, Health Hazard Data, had indicated the effects of overexposure as "Dizziness, initially, loss of consciousness eventually" and advised the emergency procedure, "Remove to fresh air." In Section VIII, Special Protection Information, under the subcategory of Respiratory Protection, was written, "If used in confined area, mask with separate air supply" and under the subcategory of Eye Protection, was written, "Desirable, where liquid may be splashed into eyes." Under the subcategory, Ventilation, was written, "Spray Booth Preferred." In Section IX, Special Precautions, the manufacturer wrote, "Cleaner exerts drying action on skin, leading to irritation. Wipe off promptly."

On the front of the can (Figure 9-3) was the name of the product in large letters, followed by "Cleaner/Remover," plus its identifying code number in slightly smaller letters.

On the back side of the container were two sections of almost equal size, one captioned "Warning," and the other, "Directions," as shown in Figure 9-4.

Unlike the FDA requirements concerning tampons, the ANSI requirements for this product, cited earlier and adopted by OSHA, did not explicitly include the requirement to be written in language that is understandable to the average consumer. Nor did they specify any particular order to the information they required. It is not clear why such requirements occur with one category of product but not with another. Perhaps it was assumed by ANSI that such practice is to be expected. In any case,

Cleaner/Remover
(Identifying code)

Formulated to meet sulfur and halogen requirements
for NAVSHIPS 250-1500-1, MIL-1-25135, ASTM E 165
ASMF-V, RDT 3-6T

Contains No Fluorocarbon Propellants

Net Weight 13 ounces

(NAME OF COMPANY) Corporation

____

(City, State, zip code, USA)

____

Trademark Reg. U.S. Pat. Off. Marca Registrada en Mexico.

FIGURE 9-3. Cleaner/Remover (Front of Container)

these two characteristics could not then serve as the most robust basis of a complaint against the manufacturer.

On the other hand, examination of the warning reveals some significant problems. Comparing the six subjects required in ANSI's paragraph 3.2, we find:

ANSI Paragraph 3.2	Container label
1. Identity of product or hazardous component(s)	Contains: Methyl Chloroform
2. Signal word	Warning
3. Statement of hazards	Material can be hazardous to health if not used according to instructions. Contents under pressure.
4. Precautionary measures	Use only in well ventilated area. Avoid contact with eyes or skin and breathing of vapor or spray mist.

Warning: **Material can be hazardous to health if not used according to instructions. Contents under pressure.**

Contains: Methyl Chloroform.
Use only in well ventilated area.
Avoid contact with eyes or skin and breathing of vapor or spray mist.
In case of contact with eyes flood repeatedly with water.
If swallowed, do not induce vomiting.
If overcome by vapors, remove to fresh air.
In above case call a physician immediately. Wash skin with soap and water.
Do not puncture, incinerate or store above 120° (48.8° C).
For industrial use by qualified personnel only.
Not for household use.
Keep out of reach of children.

Directions: **Cleaner/Remover**
(COMPANY NAME)
Cleaner/Remover is intended for use with (Trade Name) and (Trade Name) penetrant system and other (COMPANY NAME) Corporation test methods and materials

Use As A Precleaner:
To be used as a precleaner to remove oily residues. Apply directly to test area, wipe clean. Allow test area to dry before further processing.

Use As A Penetrant Remover:
To be used as a penetrant remover; apply Cleaner/Remover to clean cloth and wipe excess penetrant from surface. Repeat until surface is free of penetrant.
Do Not Flush Surface With Remover As Sensitivity May Be Impaired.

Label No: 4-3751-11

FIGURE 9-4. **Cleaner/Remover (Back of Container)**

5. Instructions in case of contact or exposure	In case of contact with eyes flood repeatedly with water. If swallowed, do not induce vomiting.
6. Antidotes	If overcome by vapors, remove to fresh air. In above cases call a physician immediately. Wash skin with soap and water.

On the surface, it may appear that the manufacturer has complied with the requirements of ANSI here. But compare what the container label says with what the manufacturer reported to OSHA on the Material Safety Data Sheet noted above.

ANSI requirement	*OSHA data sheet*	*Container*
1. Identity of hazardous components	1.1.1 Trichloroethane 97%; Carbon Dioxide 3% (re: decomposition products): Phosgene, hydrochloric acid if vapors are exposed to flame, arcs, red hot surfaces.	Methyl Chloroform
2. Signal word	Indicate the relative degree of severity in diminishing order of DANGER!, WARNING!, CAUTION! If more than one hazard, use one of greatest hazard.	Warning:
3. Statement of hazard	Dizziness, initially, loss of consciousness eventually. Cleaner exerts drying action on skin, leading to irritation.	(unspecified)
4. Precautionary measures	If used in confined area, mask with separate air supply. Spray booth preferred. (In case of spills or leaks): mop-up crew should wear respirators with absorbent canisters. (re: eye protection): desirable where liquid may be splashed into eyes. Store away from heat. Avoid using near flame, arcs, red hot surfaces.	Use only in well ventilated area. Avoid contact with eyes and skin and breathing of vapor or spray mist.
5. Instructions in case of contact or exposure	Remove to fresh air. If in eyes, rinse copiously with water.	In case of contact with eyes, flood repeatedly with water.

6. Antidotes	Remove to fresh air	If swallowed, do not induce vomiting. If overcome by vapors, remove to fresh air. In above cases, call a physician immediately. Wash skin with soap and water.

In this case I was asked to revise the warning label portion of the container to bring the language into line with OSHA requirements. This turned out to be a task in redesigning the front of the can as well as the back, since it was my opinion that any product that could cause brain damage should have DANGER written in a prominent position on the front of the can. Therefore, the revised label's front kept the same large lettered product name and the words Cleaner/Remover and changed virtually everything else, as shown in Figure 9-5.

This revision placed the signal word, "Danger," the identity of the hazardous components, the precautionary measures, and the statement of hazards in a prominent position on the container, on the front in readable print.

My revision placed the instructions in case of contact or exposure and antidotes on the back of the can, as shown in Figure 9-6.

I regard this revision as a step in the right direction but probably still not the perfect warning label. It places the hazard in a prominent position, on the front of the container, and identifies methyl chloroform as the cause of various dangers. It increases the severity of the hazard from "Warning" to "Danger," appropriate, in this case, to the effects that the product can have on a user. It also puts the precaution measures up front, in a prominent position. It marks the important instructions for first aid and antidotes clearly at the top of the back of the can. It improves the document design with added white space and bulleted series statements.

Although the ANSI guidelines do not specify the exact placement of these features, logic tells us that the following sequence is appropriate for hazards:

1. Tell what the hazard is
2. Tell how to avoid the hazard
3. Tell what to do if a person is injured by the hazard

DANGER
This product contains methyl chloroform which causes dizziness, loss of consciousness, and even death.

TO PREVENT DANGER:

- Use only in ventilated areas.
- If you use in confined areas, mask with air supply.
- Follow all directions carefully.

DO NOT: breath vapor spray or mist.
DO NOT: allow contact with eyes or skin
DO NOT: use near flames or heat
DO NOT: puncture, incinerate or store above 120° (48.8° C)

Non-Flammable

Meets sulfur and halogen requirements for NAVSHIPS 250-1500-1, MIL-1-25135, ASTM E 165, ASMF-V, RDT 3-6.T

Contains no Fluorocarbon Propellants

Net Weight 13 Ounces

(COMPANY NAME)
(address)

Trademark Reg. U.S. Pat. Off. Marca Registrada en Mexico.

FIGURE 9-5. **Revised Cleaner/Remover (Front of Container)**

The manufacturer's label had this information on it, but in no logical sequence, creating the possibility of user confusion or negligence. The people who wrote the ANSI requirements must not have thought about the importance of sequence in communicating information about hazardous mate-

First Aid:	**If user becomes dizzy or unconscious:** **• provide fresh air immediately** **• call physician immediately** **If user swallows the product:** **• call physician immediately**	**• Do not induce vomiting.** **If product touches your eyes or skin:** **• flood eyes immediately with water** **• wash skin with soap and water** **• call physician immediately**
Directions:	**Cleaner/Remover** (company name) Cleaner/Remover is intended for use with (trade name) penetrant systems, and other (company name) test methods and materials. For industrial use by qualified personnel only. Not for household use Keep out of reach of children. **Use as a pre-cleaner** to remove oily residues. Apply to test area, wipe clean	with cloth. Repeat until clean. Allow test area to dry before further processing. **Use as a penetrant remover.** Apply Cleaner/Remover on clean cloth and wipe excess penetrant from surface. Repeat until surface is free of penetrant. Do not flush surface with remover or sensitvity may be impaired.

Label No: 4-3751-11

FIGURE 9-6. **Revised Cleaner/Remover (Back of Container)**

rial, a bureaucratic oversight. Nor did they see fit to include the requirement of making this information understandable to an average user. In this regard, the FDA regulations are far more effective and appropriate.

Conclusion

Comparison of the use of language in these two cases shows that the concept of "bureaucratic language" is far too broad. Two different bureaucracies with virtually the same problems came up with quite different sets of requirements. We can learn from this, perhaps, that the hierarchies of authority within bureaucracies are too rigid to communicate effectively with each other. This is not surprising, since this situation is exactly the one that we observed at the Social Security Administration (SSA) when we first began our work there. In that situation, the SSA divisions of general counsel, policy, systems, and notice-writing had little or no cross-fertilization, leading to many internal misunderstandings about each other's power and concerns.

But this inability or unwillingness to communicate among separate divisions is probably endemic to institutions of any kind. I can recall when, years ago, I was the linguistic advisor to a large publishing company that specialized in elementary reading and language arts materials. I was regularly flown to Boston, first to meet with the reading division, then to meet with the language arts division, then to meet with the spelling division, and so on. After discovering that I was saying essentially the same things to each division separately, I informed the vice president that this was a waste of his resources. Why not get them all into the same room at the same time? He smiled at me and pointed out that these separations were useful, that they instilled competition across divisions, and, furthermore, the company was thriving the way it was. Perhaps separate bureaus feel this same sense of competition across divisions and like it better that way. To an outsider, however, it still seems like a waste not to get bureaus like FDA and OSHA together to share the same knowledge, experience, and bureaucratic language.

Unlike the case examples in the previous chapters, these two cases, involving the FDA and OSHA, do not describe lawsuits brought against a government bureaucracy by a consumer advocacy group. Here the bureaucracies are marginal to the actual litigation but central to the cause of it. The tampon manufacturer's attempt to skirt the rather clear language of the FDA regulations got that manufacturer in the stew. It should be pointed out, however, that this same manufacturer had prevailed in other similar lawsuits that did not make use of linguistic analysis of language used by both the bureaucracy and the manufacturer. In the case of the brain-damaged worker, his attorney's burden was made much more difficult, because the language of the OSHA warning label requirements was much less precise and did not specify such important aspects as sequencing of the required information, its prominence, and the comprehensibility of such information to the average consumer.

Chapter 10

What Is Bureaucratic Language and What Can Be Done About It?

To this point, I have described a number of case studies in which various types of bureaucratic language are patently evident. In most of these cases, something burst, causing outsiders to the bureaucracy to rail against it. In each case, the overt vehicle for the reactions by outsiders was economic. Class action suits and civil suits held the club of money over the heads of the alleged offenders. Motivated by a jury decision or a judge's order, the bureaucracies had no alternative but to pay for their offenses and clean up their linguistic acts to the extent that these bureaucratic language problems did not continue to be the source of recipient or consumer pain. It is a sad commentary on the effectiveness of disciplines that argue for clear writing, perhaps, that it turns out to be money, not the inner desire to write well, which seems to be the major serious motivation for language change or improvement. Linguists who deal with language planning and policy, government bureaucracies, and private businesses, may all find this instructive.

Although it is undoubtedly true that the bureaucracies have prevailed in some such suits in the past, they clearly failed in each of the cases described here. And, of course, this is why these cases prove interesting. The common thread and new dimension throughout these case studies is the presence of linguistic analysis on the side of the offended parties. As presumptuous as this may seem, the assistance of linguistic analysis remains the single most important factor. When linguists leave the safety of their academic isolation and leap into the real world that they otherwise only theorize about, they can begin to use their knowledge to help resolve real world problems. Linguists can give lectures, teach courses, reason with convincing knowledge and logic, all to little avail in the national scene unless they are willing to add their expertise to the economic club held over the offenders' heads. This suggests, of course, a continuing and growing alliance between lawyers and linguists who are motivated to bring about improvement in the human condition. Apparently, arguments using reasonable persuasion and knowledge alone are not enough, as the chapter on the conference on insurance language illustrates.

The cases described in this book have highlighted the bureaucracy's specialization of functions, adherence to fixed rules, hierarchy of authority, and system of administration marked by officialdom, red tape, and proliferation. It has also been shown that bureaucratic language is not limited to government agencies, extending as it does to such fields as insurance, real estate, car sales, and manufacturing of products. But whether in government or industry, these bureaucratic characteristics appear to prevail. Governments tend to be bigger than business or industry, however, and this may account for the general association of such language with government bureaucracies alone. These cases also make it clear that there is no such thing as a single or unified "bureaucratic language." Indeed, there are many bureaucratic languages. Not all bureaucracies use language the same way or even agree on individual terms.

To this point, however, we have not attempted to determine what human characteristics underlie the features of these bureaucratic languages. This issue will be a consideration in what follows. Note that some of the following characteristics are described with the verb, "is," while others use the verb, "seem." This distinction is intentional. It is definitive that bureaucratic language is a mark of group membership, that it is contagious, and that it is evasive. But the other characteristics, the ones that use the verb, "seem," are ones that are unfortunate impressions given by the use of bureaucratic language, but are not necessarily its defining features. It is in these characteristics that bureaucracies can do a better job of dispelling the negative impression of the public. It is also in these areas that bureaucracies can do better in their use of clear, comprehensible, accurate language.

What Is Bureaucratic Language?

1. Bureaucratic language is a mark of membership.

One of the characteristics of jargon is that it is understood by the inside group that uses it habitually but often incomprehensible to outsiders. In this sense, bureaucratic language is similar to jargon. It is not surprising that newcomers to the field of medicine, law, dentistry, business, education, and other fields are marked as insiders only when they have managed to learn to talk and write like other more experienced members of their field. Thus doctors in training take it as a sign of their membership in the profession if they can use language like a doctor. The same is true for law students and the other groups noted above. There is nothing wrong with this *per se*. Over the years, in fact, I have learned that the best graduate students in linguistics are those who, early in their education, learn to think, write, and talk like linguists. The problem of any profession in this regard is not so much how language is used internally but in how language is used to outsiders.

Bureaucrats are no different from anyone else in this regard. They may well be measured for promotion by the extent to which they come to sound and look like others who are experts in their fields. As was noted in the case studies in this book, there are specialized bureaucratic languages common to agencies like Social Security, Medicare, the Food and Drug Administration, and the OSHA, in the fields of car sales, real estate, medicine, and insurance; among administrative hearing officers; on manufacturers' warning labels, and in many other fields. Although it was not within the scope of this book, one might easily include the bureaucratic language of law enforcement officers, attorneys, teachers, accountants, and a multitude of other areas as well.

Each specialized language is more than mere specialized vocabulary. As noted earlier, it also includes syntax, semantics, document design, schemas, and perspective-taking. Learning to use language in this way is the mark of internal membership not unlike wearing a uniform or carrying a clip board.

In a way, asking inside members of a group to give up their signs of such membership is asking quite a bit. They have worked hard to learn this language, they use it daily on the inside, and have a decreasing awareness that there is another way to talk and write. The larger and more isolated the in-group, the less likely it is that these insiders hear or see any other language than their own. Eventually, they begin to believe that it is, indeed, the only language, and that outsiders probably understand it as well as they do. In such cases, bureaucratic language becomes more than a mark of membership; it becomes thought of as the only language in town.

2. Bureaucratic language is contagious.

When a specific form of language is first heard by people one respects, it is only natural to emulate it. New catch phrases move in and out of our daily conversation in this way. President Clinton, in the campaign debates with Senator Dole in 1996, used the Arkansas expression, "I don't think that dog will hunt," meaning that a certain idea probably wouldn't work. That expression was then picked up by many people, immediately expanding its domain far beyond its Arkansas origins, at least for a while. Such contagion is at the root of language change.

It is only natural for newcomers to a particular bureaucracy to pick up the inside words quickly from their colleagues. This does not signal on their part any special effort to be arcane or uncommunicative to the world outside that bureaucracy. Critics of bureaucracies often feel that the insiders are trying deliberately to be unclear when there are predictable and natural reasons for this.

3. Bureaucratic language seems to be evasive.

On the other hand, insiders to bureaucracies can also use language to camouflage their message deliberately, particularly when trying to avoid saying something unpleasant or uncomfortable. Giving bad news is seldom easy. Physicians find it especially difficult to tell patients that they have a terminal illness. Bosses often find it hard to utter the words that fire an employee. Children are uncomfortable explaining a bad report card to their parents. There is no reason to believe that a bureaucracy is any different in this regard. It seems to be a human problem, not just a bureaucratic one.

Although it is natural to have difficulty in giving bad news, there is little justification for bureaucracies to be evasive about giving good or neutral news. As the cases described in this book illustrate, this is exactly what often happens. Congress orders the Social Security Administration (SSA) to tell recipients that they might be entitled to more benefits than they are now getting (obviously good news), and the resulting notice seems to be hiding, rather than presenting, this message. But, as we discovered in the training program that grew out of that lawsuit, the problem was not so much SSA's evasiveness as it was its inability to communicate effectively. It can be dangerous to ascribe the intention of being deliberately evasive when the root of the apparent evasiveness is actually a lack of competence or effort in using language effectively.

This does not get the bureaucracy off the hook, however. Saint Paul once wisely advised, "avoid the very appearance of evil." If the message sent by the bureaucracy can be interpreted as deliberately evasive even though this was not the intent, the same problem exists. Bureaucracies have been weak in discovering their readers' perspectives, as has been documented by many of the cases described in this book. The problem of seeming to be evasive can be resolved by consciously striving to see how the recipients might read or, perhaps more importantly, misread, what the bureaucracy is tying to say.

The curious parallel to legislation is apparent here. Law makers work very hard to make the wording of laws such that no possible misunderstanding or misreading can take place. A cursory view of litigation history shows how difficult such an effort can be. One major problem in the drafting of such laws is the failure to take the readers' perspective. Law makers often give the appearance of taking only their own perspective about the law, protecting their own intent against misreading or misunderstanding. They often fail to take into consideration the possible intent, possible schema, and possible context of the receivers of this message, resulting in unnecessary and expensive litigation that otherwise could have been avoided.

4. Bureaucratic language seems self-protective.

Self-protection is a natural human instinct, and it is only natural that organizations will take on this individual, human quality. This is not a bad thing, of course, since bureaucracies might otherwise fall apart. The problem comes when bureaucracies, like individual humans, become so absorbed in self-protection that they lose sight of their mission and purpose. Even the most self-protective human beings make mistakes and need to change their behavior in light of new circumstances and events. Admitting such problems, even admitting mistakes, is not easy. The car dealership described earlier refused to admit its mistakes from the time the lawsuit was brought against it to the very end of the trial, when the jury ruled against it. Although this kind of self-protective unity might be considered admirable loyalty in some circumstances, it was expensive and unnecessary folly in this case.

In sharp contrast to the car dealership, the Social Security Administration eventually came to admit that it had a serious problem that needed to be fixed. The agency did so in a somewhat humbling manner, admitting that the notice presented by the National Senior Citizens Law Center was superior to their own and then going the next step as well—co-opting the opposition's expert to give it the help it needed. The interesting thing about SSA's action here is that this bureaucracy did not suffer from admitting its error. Indeed, SSA's reputation with the public was the better for it. There was no need to try to avoid any public criticism. There was already plenty of this to go around, and it was inescapable. SSA simply recognized the problem, admitted it, and did something about it.

Nevertheless, bureaucracies give the impression of being overly self-protective. In an age when the very word, "bureaucracy," conjures up negative, if not hostile, feelings among by the general public, perhaps this is their inevitable hair shirt.

5. Bureaucratic language seems selfish.

Anyone who has lived for any length of time in Washington, D.C. has come to know bureaucrats personally. Some may evidence qualities that are less than desirable but, on the whole, they are really no different from the rest of the population. Many, if not most, in fact, are unselfish, hard-working, well-intentioned, kind, intelligent people who try to do their jobs as best they can. The public image of bureaucrats, foisted upon us primarily by politicians who base their forthcoming elections on "running against Washington," seems to be that government bureaucracies are wasteful and inefficient sump holes of ignorance and heartlessness. Although some of the cases cited in this book focus on the ineffectiveness of the efforts of various Washington bureaucracies to accomplish specific tasks of language use, this ineffectiveness should not be interpreted as intentional.

The public image of governmental bureaucratic selfishness may have its origins in the process of budgeting and politics that is common in government. Agencies have to compete with other agencies for funding allotments in a process that is little understood by the average person. Fighting for a budget (or existence) can give the impression of selfishness, whereas it is probably more related to the human need for self-preservation discussed earlier. It is not difficult for the public to then assume that this need to survive in the midst of agency competition and wrangling between political parties carries over to selfishness of the agencies toward the people the bureaucracy is mandated to serve.

Once again, in all my involvements with various governmental bureaucracies in my thirty years in Washington, I cannot say that the individual bureaucrats I dealt with were actually selfish. The language used by these agencies may give the impression of selfishness and unwillingness to share their resources or information with their constituents, but this impression stems largely from an ineffectiveness in communicating with their constituents. Again, language is at the core of the problem.

6. Bureaucratic language seems rigid.

Because of real or imagined forces motivating it, bureaucratic language seems impenetrable to modification. The real forces are, of course, the law and regulations that government bureaucrats begin with, and the company or professional rules that control and encourage bureaucratic language in the business and professional worlds. Rigidity, of course, is nourished by power, a natural enemy of language change. The power of those in authority can instill a kind of hopelessness in those whose job it is to carry out orders without question.

Such was the situation we originally found among the notice-writers at the Social Security Administration. Those who had worked there longest were the most pessimistic about changing the system, but even the newcomers had begun to be discouraged about their work. It did not take long for us to determine that the most serious impediments to clear writing were the notice-writers' hopelessness and the lack of power they felt to present or defend their good ideas about what a notice ought to look like. We first tried to identify and defuse the source of their hopelessness, which they described as the rigidity of the system in which law, policy, and the computer capability all conspired to make them write the way they did. We then tried to fortify them with the power of language analysis which would give them powerful justifications for the changes they proposed. They were, in essence, fighting a battle against an imagined enemy with no real weapons.

Change from within is one way to attack bureaucratic rigidity. Change from without is another way. By the latter I refer to consumer rights groups such as the National Senior Citizens Law Center, that bring class action suits against various bureaucracies in an effort to bring them to their knees. In a sense, the civil law cases in the areas of the real estate and car sales bureaucracies are similar in this respect. Perhaps the least effective attack on bureaucratic rigidity described in this book is the one exemplified by the conference on insurance language, where experts and representatives spoke their piece, then went back to the same apparent rigidity from whence they came.

The fact that the attacks on bureaucratic language have prevailed, from efforts both within and without, suggests, however, that such rigidity is not as fixed or permanent as one might suspect. Thus, I do not place the characteristic of rigidity in the same definitive category as a mark of membership, contagion, or evasiveness. These cannot be expected to change, although improvements certainly can be made in how they are communicated. There is considerable hope for changing the appearance of rigidity, at least under the right conditions. And once the appearance is changed, the reality might well follow.

What Can Be Done About Bureaucratic Language?

Bureaucratic language will not go away easily, if at all. But its excesses can be trimmed a bit with a few judicious decisions. I make no claim that we have all the answers to this problem, but by examining a number of different bureaucracies in a number of different settings, certain similarities emerge. If the current state of bureaucratic language is to be improved, outsiders to these bureaucracies will need to take an active role. One cannot expect bureaucracies to police themselves. Such actions include, but are not limited to, the following:

1. Carry a big stick.

I have emphasized the economic motivation for change throughout this book. The class action and civil lawsuits described here make it clear that this, unfortunately, is probably the best hammer to hold over the head of a bureaucracy. I have not focused on the bureaucracy of medicine here, but recent developments in this field can be instructive. Linguists have tried, since the seventies, to convince the medical profession that it would benefit by paying more attention to the language used in medical interviews (Shuy 1976, 1977). Even though such medical journals as the *New England Journal of Medicine* pointed out that 95% of success of treatment depends on getting accurate information from the patient (Mechanic 1972), such suggestions were met with either silence or objections about there being no room in the curriculum for such matters.

Recently, new research has shown that the way doctors communicate with patients during routine visits seems to affect the chances of an ensuing malpractice suit. Doctors who spend more time with their patients, encourage patients to talk and ask questions, and help patients understand what is going on during their treatment, are less likely to be sued.

This finding is significant in a number of ways. For one thing, it shows that the threat of economic penalty seems to capture the attention of the profession, while the earlier research findings demonstrating the effectiveness of improved doctor-patient communication seems to have little effect. Apparently a good idea that suggests change is not a good idea unless avoiding it costs something. There is an entropy in bureaucracies that seems to say, "If it ain't broke, don't fix it." One strong way to show that it is broken is to threaten a lawsuit. This is, indeed, unfortunate. It is not the hope of this book to encourage litigation. But bureaucracies, such as medicine, noted specifically here, as well as government and business, can learn from carrying a big stick, the threat of lawsuits, as much as from the lawsuits themselves. The big stick gets the attention of the offending bureaucracy in ways which have otherwise been ineffective.

2. Improve communication within bureaucracies.

Once the bureaucracy's attention is gained, the next step is to help. In conventional lawsuits, one party is recompensed and the other is punished. Although there is probably no way to subvert such a process, I am suggesting something quite different here. Try desperately to get the bureaucracy to comply with linguistic reason before trial, as was done in many of the cases against government bureaucracies noted in this book. This is, indeed, the Gray Panthers' approach. Give your idea to the opposition before the trial in the hope that they will see its wisdom and appropriateness. And, of course, if this fails, give the same idea to them at trial. On some occasions, I have rewritten the offending documents for the bureaucracy more as a teaching tool than as a threat, even though all that was required was for me to show how ineffective the offending document was. Even though counsel for the bureaucracy may not be willing to concede at this point, the agency itself may learn from it, as SSA did in the case described in Chapter 2.

3. Learn to accept small gains and hope for larger ones.

I have noted several occasions in which both sides of a controversy about bureaucratic language made concessions to each other. I have not always been pleased with these negotiated conclusions, of course. But this seems to be the nature of litigation, and those who help with it, such as linguists, must learn to live with it, hoping for a next time in which to make things the way we really want them. This could be viewed as a lack of resolve on our part. I view it differently. We give it our best shot and that's about all we can do.

4. Be hopeful and optimistic.

The attitude of hopelessness that we found initially among the SSA notice-writers is not unlike the hopelessness of the general public about the bureaucratic language that is committed daily. But is the situation really hopeless? It should be clear that this book tries to argue that it is not.

The very conditions, such as specialization of functions and hierarchy of authority, used here to describe "the bureaucracy," are actually the same ones that can be applied to those who have the potential to do the most about it. I noted, for example, that bureaucracies tend to be isolated by their specializations. One agency is unacquainted with what another agency is doing. Even one branch of an agency is unacquainted with what other branches are doing. Each has its own hierarchy of authority which vies, directly or indirectly, with competing hierarchies of authority. Otherwise admirable qualities, such as loyalty and unity, tend to isolate work units from each other, leading to competition rather than to cooperation. Work overload also contributes to this isolation. In a similar way, those who might best work together to help resolve the problems caused by bureaucratic language, namely lawyers, linguists, and bureaucrats, have been equally isolated from each other.

Breaking down isolation seems to be one of the keys to improving hopefulness about bureaucratic language. In our training of SSA notice-writers, for example, we discovered that many of these well-meaning bureaucrats had never had any personal contact with actual beneficiaries. Their writing, therefore, reflected little or no sense about recipient design. The obvious answer to this was to send them out to nursing homes near their office and have them talk with real people, and not be satisfied only with written communication. In all of the training programs we conducted, this "fieldwork" experience was regarded as a highlight. The writers broke down their isolation and began to write from the beneficiaries' perspectives.

5. Join forces to work together for change.

In a similar way, linguists can be most helpful to attorneys by jumping into the fire of actual litigation and trying to see the issues from the perspective of law. This does not mean that linguists have to be advocates or take sides. Lawyers are advocates. Linguists are not, and should not try to be. The Good Samaritan gained insights into the problems of the sick beggar by walking up to him rather than crossing the street to avoid him, as the other men in the parable did. He took deliberate steps to come into contact with the issue. Simply sitting on the sidelines and speculating or theorizing is not at all like getting involved directly.

Likewise, lawyers who grapple with complex language issues may be wise to seek the company of linguists, who have an expertise that most lawyers usually do not possess. Law, by definition, is heavily involved in the analysis of language, however, and attorneys can surely benefit from the help of linguists in such matters.

It is in this joining together that progress in improving the state of bureaucratic language can best be accomplished. Bureaucracies are not likely to be able to do this alone, although, with proper training, they can do quite a bit. Nor are linguists or lawyers able to do this alone. It is toward this goal of a cooperative joining of resources that this book is offered.

Works Cited

Ballard, James C., and Susan L. Rode-Perkins. "How to Create Mass Media Print Warnings," *Technical Communication*, second quarter (1987):84–89.

Barber, Bernard. *Informed Consent in Medical Therapy and Research.* New Brunswick, N.J.: Rutgers University Press, 1986.

Davison, Alice, and Robert N. Kantor. "On the Failure of Readability Formulas to Define Readable Texts," *Reading Research Quarterly* XVII, no. 2 (1987):187–209.

Fisher, Sue. *In the Patient's Best Interest.* New Brunswick, N.J.: Rutgers University Press, 1986.

Fisher, Sue, and Alexandra Todd, eds. 3 *Discourse and Institutional Authority: Medicine, Education and Law.* Norwood, N.J.: Ablex, 1986.

Flesch, Rudolph F. *The Art of Readable Writing.* New York: Collier, 1949.

Grice, H.P. "Logic and Conversation." In *Syntax and Semantics 3*, edited by Peter Cole and Jerry Morgan 41–58. New York: Academic Press, 1975.

Halliday, Michael and Ruqaiya Hassan. *Cohesion in English.* London: Longman, 1976

Kemnitz, Charles. "How to Write Effective Hazard Alert Messages." *Technical Communication*, first quarter (1991):68–73.

Mechanic, David. "Some Psychologic Factors Affecting the Presentation of Bodily Complaints," *New England Journal of Medicine* 286 (1972):1132–1139.

Mishler, Elliot G. *The Discourse of Medicine.* Norwood, N.J.: Ablex, 1984.

Nader, Laura, and Thomas Maretski. *Cultural Illness and Health.* Washington, D.C.: American Anthropology Association, 1973.

Pear, Robert. "Administration Softens Medicare Appeals Plan," *New York Times*, 8 October 1987.

Reddish, Janice. *Guidelines for Document Designers.* Washington, D.C.: American Institutes for Research, 1981.

Schott, Gretchen H., and Patricia A. Robinson. *Writing Design Manuals*. 2nd ed. Chelsea, Michigan: Lewis Publishers, 1991.

Shuy, Roger W. The patient's right to clear communication in the medical interview. ITL, Leuven, Belgium, 1977.

—— "Topic as the Unit of Analysis in a Criminal Law Case." In *Analyzing Discourse: Text and Talk*, edited by Deborah Tannen, 113–125. Washington, D.C.: Georgetown University Press, 1982.

—— "Linguistic Analysis of Real Estate Commission Agreements in a Civil Lawsuit." In *Language Topics: Essays in Honour of Michael Halliday*, edited by Ross Steele and Terry Threadgold, 333–358. Amsterdam: John Benjamins, 1987.

——"Changing Language Policy In a Bureaucracy." In *Language Spread and Language Policy*, edited by Peter Lowenberg, 150–174. Washington, D.C.: Georgetown University Press, 1988.

—— "Warning Labels: Language, Law, and Comprehensibility," *American Speech 65.4* (1990): 291–303.

—— "Deceit, Distress, and False Imprisonment: The Anatomy of a Car Sales Event," *Forensic Linguistics* 1, no. 2 (1994): 133–149.

"Simplification of Insurance Policy Language." *New York Business*. (July/August, 1975) 170.

Tannen, Deborah. *You Just Don't Understand*. New York: Morrow, 1990.

Todd, Alexandra. *Intimate Adversaries*. Philadelphia: University of Pennsylvania Press, 1989.

U.S. General Accounting Office. "Medicare Claims: HCFA Proposal to Establish an Administrative Law Judge Unit," U.S. General Accounting Office, Briefing Report to Congressional Committees, April 1988.

U.S. Office of Consumer Affairs. *Consumers and Life Insurance - An Exchange of Views*. Washington, D.C.: U.S. Office of Consumer Affairs, May 1978.

United States Court of Appeals for The District of Columbia Circuit. 79-1603, Gray Panthers, et. al., V. Richard S. Schweiker, Secretary of The Department of Health and Human Services (D.C. Civil Action No. 77-0488), March 18, 1981

United States District Court for The District of Columbia, (Civil No. 77-488), Defendant's Proposed Plan Re: Courts Order of May 21, 1981, July 17, 1981.

West, Candace, *Routine Complications*. Bloomington: Indiana University Press, 1989.

Index

active vs. passive voice, 113–115
address forms, 73, 74, 91, 98, 104
adherence to fixed rules, 150–153
ambiguity, 113
anaphora, 116, 126–127
American National Standards Institute (ANSI), 159–174
attorney hearings, 71–72
authority based on linguistic justification, 43–44
avoiding displays of knowledge, 94–96, 98, 101–102

bad news, 178
Barber, Bernard, 53
Bein, Mitchell, 145–157
beneficiaries' perspective, 16–18, 92–93, 98, 101–102
biological differentiation, 105–106
bureaucratic language defined, 176–181
bureaucratic perspective, 14

capitalization, 10, 11
car sales language, 144–157
causal relationships, 42
challenges, 78–81
Clear Writing Staff of SSA, 24, 26, 46
Clinton, William J., 178
cohesion, 40–41
cooperative principle, 29, 95, 103
colloquial vs. predictable, 116–118
commission agreement language, 125–143
comprehensibility, 113
communicative interaction, 15
communicative turn, 15
corollary topics, 138–140
consumer's perspective, 14
contextual constraints, 43
contractions, 74, 98
contrastive analysis, 140–142
conversational style, 73, 92, 100
conversational turn, 16
conveyed meaning, 51

Davison, Alice, 116
decision tree, 34–35
defusing the legal format, 89–92, 100–101
denying, 46

dependent clauses, 50
directives, 57
discourse analysis, 39, 40, 137
Doggett, Jr., Herbert R., 24
Dole, Robert, 178

embedding, 50
ethnographic study, 68
explicitness, 122

face threatening, 92, 93, 99
face to face interaction, 14
feedback markers, 73, 75–76, 91, 98, 104
Fisher, Sue, 53
Flesch, Rudolph, 110–112

gender differences, 73–106
given-new principle, 118
giving the bad news, 47
Goldberg v. Kelly, 64
Grice, H.P., 39, 41

Halliday, Michael, 40
Hanson, J. Ross, 109–112, 116
Hassan, Ruqaiya, 40
Health Care Financing Administration (HCFA), 65
hierarchy of authority, 153–154

indirectness, 73, 76–77, 98
indirect speech acts, 36
inferencing, 118–119
in-person hearings, 63, 66–107
insurance policy language, 108–123
intonation, 73, 76, 98, 104

jargon, 10, 121
Johnson, Michael, 145–146

Kantor, Robert, 111
Kennedy, Edward, 2
Kilpatrick, James J., 50

Lamberth, Royce C., 7
Legal Services of Middle Tennessee, 53–62
lexical cohesion, 40
limited inventory, 120–121

Maretski, Thomas, 53
maxims, 39–40
McDonald, Ron, 109
McSteen, Martha, 24–25, 30
Mechanic, David, 182
Medicare Act, 1–4, 78
Medical Benefits Notice, 4–18
Miranda warnings, 100
misconceptions about language, 119–123
Mishler, Elliot G., 57
mitigated warnings, 100

Nader, Laura, 53
National Safety Council (NSC), 159
National Senior Citizens Law Center (NSCLC), 1–4, 8, 11, 14, 17, 19–24, 46, 62–65, 107, 179, 181, 183
negative speech acts, 38–39
neutral speech acts, 38–39
nominalization, 9, 115–116
non-verbal cues, 91, 98
Notice of Medicare Claim Determination, 46–51
Notice Review Guide, 45

officialdom, red tape and proliferation, 154–157
opinion survey, 66–67
Overby, Russ, 54

paper hearing, 1, 14, 17
performatives, 33
personal comments, 74–75, 98
personal pronouns, 83–85, 99
Peterson, Esther, 109
Physician's Disability Report Form, 53–62
physician hearings, 70–71
physical presence, 106–107
positive speech acts, 38–39
power, 69–70, 81–88, 92, 98–99
prepositions, 50
print type, 10
public perspective, 14, 152

question types, 88, 91

readability, 10, 49–51, 110
readability formulas, 43, 49–50, 109–112
reader's perspective, 32
recipient compliance, 56
recipient design, 92
recipient perspective, 12, 51
Reddish, Janice, 42
register, 73, 97–98, 102
repetition, 117–118, 121
Richardson, Lee, 109
Roper, William L., 64–65
Ruff, Charles F.C., 7

Schnakenberg, Barbara, 24
Schweiker, Richard, 1
self-generated topics, 88–89, 92, 98–100
semantic network, 161–162
Shuy, Roger W., 109, 138, 146, 164, 182
simplicity vs. clarity, 109–112, 120
sincere conditions, 36
Social Security Administration (SSA), 2–9, 19–45, 47, 53–57, 65, 174, 177, 179, 181, 183–184
Social Security Award Certificate, 30
sociolinguistics, 68
specialization of functions, 146–149
speech acts, 34–39, 46, 73, 92
Staton, Jana J., 25–28, 32–33
status and role, 70–72, 74
structure of a car sales event, 147–149
structural framework of the hearing, 89–92
substantive topics, 138–140
Supplementary Security Income (SSI), 19–45
synonymy, 111–112
Sweeney, Eileen P., 23–24

tampon warning statements, 159–165
Tannen, Deborah, 90
technical terms, 91
telephonic hearing, 14, 17, 63, 67–107
Tennessee Disability Determination Section (TDDS), 53–62
terms of art, 43, 51, 121
Texas Deceptive Trade Practices Act, 146
Texas Human Resources Code, 146
Thompson, Lawrence H., 65
Todd, Alexandra, 53
tone, 35
topic analysis, 31–33
topic-comment, 137–140
toxic shock syndrome (TSS), 160–165

U.S. Department of Health and Human Services (HHS), 1–19
U.S. Department of Labor, Occupational Safety and Health Administration (OSHA), 165, 167, 174, 177
U.S. Food and Drug Administration (FDA), 47, 158–165, 173, 177
U.S. General Accounting Office (GAO), 65
U.S. Office of Consumer Affairs, 108

vocabulary, 51

warning labels, 158–174
West, Candace, 53
Wilson, Sally Hart, 47, 49
winning vs. losing, 85–88
Woodward, III, William, 109
word comprehension, 42
word level vs. discourse level clarity, 116–118